A Kind of Prospero

Sebastian Walker
1942-1991

Watercolour of Sebastian in a fantastic woodland by
Binette Schroeder, 1976

A Kind of Prospero

Sebastian Walker
1942-1991

MIRABEL CECIL

WALKER BOOKS
AND SUBSIDIARIES
LONDON • BOSTON • SYDNEY

ACKNOWLEDGEMENTS

*I acknowledge with thanks everyone
who talked to me about Sebastian;
their names appear throughout these pages.
And to others who gave me background
material, I am also deeply indebted.
Without their recollections, written and
verbal, this book could not
have been written.
I would like to give special thanks to
Jenny Moores, who so generously gave her
time and energy to tracking down pictures –
a treasure hunt whose reward is seen
throughout these pages, which have been so
beautifully designed by Amelia Edwards.*

M.C.

Contents

"Our worlds were two different planets,

and beyond a love of music and a handful of friends

in common, nothing bound us to each other yet

I thought of him always, as I think of him now,

with enormous affection and respect.

Now and then he gave the impression that there were

whole areas to human feeling and experience with

which one could not possibly have expected him to engage:

how ironic this now seems in view of all those of us

whose lives he enriched by his shrewd intuitions

as to what would make us happy!"

– Jonathan Keates, August 1991

*Mirabel and Sebastian
on holiday as children,
c. 1950*

Introduction

Soon after my brother Sebastian Walker died, in June 1991, I began to interview his friends and go through his papers – he kept every scrap of paper, including school reports and telephone messages – in order to commemorate the life of a remarkable man and a brilliant publisher and, for my own part, to try to reconcile the many paradoxes of his nature.

He was not, for example, the only publisher who never read, but it was odd for a tycoon who strenuously advocated childhood literacy to affect to despise grown-up books, pitying their authors (of whom I was one) as deluded fools who spent years and years creating something which few people wanted and for which they would get paid almost nothing (that is, compared with his authors, of course).

Sebastian made a great deal of money – which he loved spending: as far as my family and I were concerned he was the most generous of men – but his house was furnished with an almost spartan simplicity; no rich man's baubles there. In his wardrobe hung tailor-made suits and shirts, but what he wore most were simple dark trousers and a white open-necked shirt.

Walker Books, which he started in 1978, was central to his life. It would not have been the success it was had it been otherwise, and yet Sebastian spent a considerable part of every working day playing the piano, starting in the morning and returning to it in the early evening. Although impatient by nature, he never grudged the time he spent at the keyboard going over a passage, a phrase, a single chord. He was obsessive, obstinate, a perfectionist in this as in everything else. His relationship with his chosen instrument was the only one in his life which gave him unadulterated pleasure; the piano was the one companion of which he never tired.

Sebastian was a solitary. Yet he loved his friends, of whom he had a great many, and one could say that he actually craved affection. "You could enjoy a tremendous friendship with him," said Maurice Sendak, who did, "but you always knew exactly when the door was shut, and you didn't dare trespass. We had a very good relationship, respecting each other, but you couldn't cross the line, you got a frigid little look around the eyes and you knew that that was it, and you wondered why he didn't invite you in more.

"Well, that was his problem. Someone said he wasn't capable of love or passion, and I said there are endless variations of love and passion, they just take different forms, and you are silly to think Sebastian was incapable of them."

The central paradox of his character was that for all his forceful personality, his success in creating Walker Books, his love of music and opera, his sophistication, his many friends and his devoted staff, underlying these one had the feeling that Sebastian had very little sense of his own identity. Alongside the shrewd figure with his sure instinct for the market was a small and solitary boy.

Mirabel Cecil

August 1995

Childhood

Sebastian's success as a publisher and businessman surprised his friends from school and university who remembered him as frivolous, intelligent, but with no discernible ambition or commercial talent, let alone the determination and energy which drove him at Walker Books.

In fact both his father and his grandfather were successful entrepreneurial businessmen: his father, Richard Walker, was the managing director of a light engineering firm, Walker Crosweller, started by *his* father in 1921. Sebastian's maternal grandfather was City Engineer for Oxford before his premature death in the late 1920s, his health undermined by serving in the First World War. His daughter, Christine, Sebastian's mother, was his only, adored child.

Sebastian was born in 1942 in Cheltenham. As a boy he was sweet-natured and affectionate, with thick brown curls, wide-apart brown eyes and an endearing grin. His only sibling, I was born eighteen months after him. Our parents lived in a flat in a modern block in the centre of Cheltenham, with a large communal garden. Like most families of their sort they employed a nanny, in fact a series of nannies in uniforms with starched collars and cuffs, all of whom I remember affectionately. These gave way as we got older to au pairs. But our parents played the main part in our young lives. Our father was keen on gardening and we often used to go and play by the allotment where he grew flowers, fruit and vegetables. Occasionally we would drive out into the Cotswolds; fresh produce, such as eggs and butter, was scarce after the War and we could buy them straight from the farms, but in general Sebastian never became particularly interested in the wonderful Cotswold countryside that surrounded the town. He was no more enthusiastic about the sea: our father was a keen sailor and holidays were spent in Devon or Cornwall, where he kept his boat for many years, a six-ton Bermuda sloop, all wood, brass and canvas.

Although ours was not an especially bookish household, we were brought up on all the current childhood heroes: Orlando and Babar in their satisfyingly outsize formats; Rupert Bear; Kipling; not, alas, E. Nesbit, but *The Wind in the Willows*. Later on Sebastian's resemblance to Mr Toad was remarked on by many for his fantasizing, his boasting, for loving the latest speedy vehicle, in Toad's case a motor-car, in Sebastian's a helicopter, and for getting into scrapes and having to be got out of them by devoted friends and relations. Enid Blyton's books, from Noddy to the Famous Five, were devoured.

As he grew up it was his other engineering grandfather, James Walker, whose strong personality influenced Sebastian. He was a difficult man, particularly in personal relationships, as husband or father, an autocrat with strongly expressed views, but he was innovative, unafraid and individual – and he enjoyed his clever grandson's company. From an early age Sebastian felt at home with him. He admired, and was slightly shocked by, his grandfather's ruthlessness in business.

James Walker had always been enterprising: he had gone to Manchester Grammar School on a scholarship and then to Salford Technical College. His own father was a foundry manager, but instead of going into engineering directly he had preferred to sell advertising space. When he had first married his good-looking, dark-haired Lancastrian wife at the turn of the century they had lived in furnished rooms, not having the money for anywhere of their own. His break came when he suggested to the distinguished editor of *The Manchester Guardian*, C.P. Scott, the idea of an engineering page, for which he sold advertising space. Just before the First World War he was successful enough to be able to move out to the prosperous suburb of Wilmslow in Cheshire with his growing family. He started his own advertising agency in London and attracted many prestigious accounts, but his biggest enterprise was starting an engineering business with a partner in 1921.

James Walker,
Sebastian's grandfather,
c. 1937, aged 60

This was in Bermondsey in the East End of London. Slowly Walker Crosweller began to make a profit, until in 1936 he moved it to the country town of Cheltenham: here it was installed in a purpose-built factory, with playing fields, looking across to hills and the surrounding countryside. It manufactured thermostatic controls, shower valves and fittings.

It was his entrepreneurial grandfather who encouraged in Sebastian the idea that he should be the third generation of the family to go into the business, an idea of continuity which tends to appeal to the older generation, especially when they are the ones responsible for founding the business. Sebastian was drawn to James Walker's liberal, not to mention Bohemian, outlook. He and his wife ceased living together in 1931 (she was every bit as outspoken and assertive as he was) but he was fond of women and it was not long before he had a new female companion whom he met during the course of another of his progressive activities – nudism.

At the nudist colony he went to in Hertfordshire everyone had soubriquets to conceal their identity while the rest of them was totally revealed: his was Dek, his new lady's was Mélisande, after Pelleas and Mélisande; this was shortened to Mel, a nickname which stuck, in preference to her real name, which was Sylvia Bull.

For the next thirty-five years, until his death in 1963, Mel was James' devoted companion. (They did not marry until shortly before he died.) Sebastian was genuinely attached to this prosaic woman, visited her when she was widowed, and mourned her when she died, partly out of loyalty to his grandfather's memory, partly because the rest of the family regarded her as a bit of a joke, but mainly because he loved her, more spontaneously than he loved most people.

Sylvia Bull, James Walker's second wife, known as Mel, after Mélisande, her soubriquet in the naturist colony in Hertfordshire where they met in the 1930s

Our mother was very musical, the piano stood prominently in the drawing-room, and we both had lessons from an early age. She was also a Francophile, spoke the language fluently and had great feeling for the country. Sebastian shared both these enthusiasms, in fact his first visit to France on an exchange to Annecy in 1957, when he was fifteen, changed his life, providing him with a second family, the Davignons, a second language – he was soon bilingual – and a second country, not to mention an inexhaustible love of French food. For the rest of his life he returned regularly to the Davignons' house, Les Mirabelles (named after the old plum tree in the garden), in the Avenue du Stand in old Annecy. Renée Davignon, sharp-eyed and astringent, was a teacher of Latin, her husband a middle-ranking local government official. They and their four children took immediately to the clever English schoolboy with his quick ear for French and willingness to join in with their way

of life. To Sebastian his summer visit to Annecy was golden; I remember how impressed he was by the amount which the French spent on food and wine compared with the English. He even manifested an uncharacteristic penchant for climbing in the surrounding Savoie mountains wearing khaki shorts and a dark beret acquired locally.

Sebastian the schoolboy in grey flannel regulation suit on exeat from Rugby with his mother, mid-1950s

Sebastian's education was conventional enough: his first school, a friendly kindergarten run by two devoted unmarried ladies, was followed by the Junior School of Cheltenham College and then he was sent away to board at Rugby School.

As he was not a healthy child, but afflicted throughout his boyhood with bronchitis and other

19

chest complaints, as well as asthma, the decision to send him away to this rigorous public school may seem hard; but ours was a family where education counted above everything and there were no local schools as good as Rugby.

He coasted through his time there doing no more, but no less, than he had to, until his last year, when he really made an effort in order to get into Oxford: "He showed no seeds of promise at Rugby," says his housemaster, James Hunt.

His nickname at Rugby, "Hatty" Walker, which followed him from his prep school, was given him on account of the elaborate hats our mother used to wear, confections of flowers or fruit or feathers which were a conspicuous feature of the Sunday chapel services.

Sebastian's boarding house, Sherriff House, was one of the most civilized in Rugby. That this was so was largely due to its remarkable housemaster and his wife, James and Catherine Hunt. The house itself, named after the founder of the school, was comparatively modern, having been built only twenty-five years before, at a cost of £60,000, by a pupil of Lutyens, whose influence is evident in the tall chimneys, the long dormer windows and the steeply pitched roof. Downstairs there were parquet floors and a handsome dining-room with a hammer-beam ceiling. The main school close by was largely built by Butterfield "in a Victorian Gothic style which doesn't lift the spirits much, with its over-elaboration of decoration and of detail," says Nicholas Montagu, who was Sebastian's close friend at school and at Oxford.

When James Hunt, a classicist, had been appointed house-master, in 1955, the year before Sebastian went to Rugby, the house had an unsavoury atmosphere. "When I went through to the boys' side the house smelt of sex," he remembered. "There were nude pin-ups in their studies." The Hunts and their family of four children instilled something more civilized. Mrs Hunt ate lunch with the boys, who were expected to make conversation.

She made sure the food was adequate, buying the supplies herself from the wholesaler; and she put fresh flowers about the house.

There was beating, but James Hunt says that he disliked it: "I would never beat for bad work." It is unlikely that Sebastian was ever beaten. There was fagging – running messages and doing chores for older boys – which worked quite well because both sides got something out of it. As for homosexuality, it was an integral part of boarding-house life: "The school combined macho values with the usual hothouse boarding school sexuality," according to Nick Montagu.

Rugby guaranteed a good education but not a good time. It was down-to-earth, a bit grim, a "manly" school where sport predominated, especially, of course, the rugby football which originated there. In Sebastian's time games were compulsory three times a week, rugby and hockey in the winter and spring, and cricket in the summer. Fives was a good soft option. "Corps" (army training) was also compulsory, which Sebastian loathed and made no effort at. "He became like the comic soldier, he rebelled overtly," says Nick Montagu. "Just as people who are fat become clowns to defend themselves against attack, so Sebastian turned himself into someone completely outrageous to disarm attack because his values were not Rugby's." He sent it up and himself with it. There was a fair amount of fooling around, notably at the house suppers when the boys did "turns": for a take-off of the Oxford interviews Sebastian borrowed a piece of gold damask which he draped round him so as to show one bare shoulder and stuck an artificial rose behind his ear. "He looked enormously sexy!" says Mrs Hunt.

Sebastian tolerated Rugby and was often happy there despite its philistine atmosphere. (Even his friendship with Nick Montagu was against the ethos of the school because boys were expected to make friends within their own year, and Nick was two years younger than Sebastian.)

"He was out of place but I don't think he was unhappy," says Nick now. "He worked out a way of compromising between the school's values and his own"; besides which Mr Hunt had enough imagination to make allowances for individuals within the system, recognizing that not all of his charges were overwhelmingly interested in games. Sebastian was in the architectural section of the natural history society which involved trips to large houses. As his voice did not break until fairly late, he sang in the choir and in quartets as a treble for many years. He played the piano throughout his time there. As for work, he did the minimum until his last year, when he specialized, and shone, in subjects he wanted to do, French and History. In his last school report his housemaster said, "There is a champagne quality about his enthusiasm which we shall sadly miss … he has been great fun." His piano teacher wrote that she was sure his playing "will always give him pleasure". So Sebastian's later claims to have hated Rugby and been thoroughly unhappy there are at odds with these contemporary accounts and reports of his schooldays. It was not the ideal school for him, but he managed to avoid its heartier aspects and got a lot out of it − as much as any schoolboy with no particular inclination towards work. He worked hard enough to gain a place at New College, Oxford, where he went in 1961, reading not French or History, as might have been expected, but Politics, Philosophy and Economics.

Family photographs: (top left) Sebastian's parents on their wedding day 1937; (below left) Sebastian and Mirabel with their mother, and (right) on holiday at the seaside with their father

At Oxford, Sebastian discovered various things he really enjoyed – Society, the grander the better, and entertaining, of which he never tired. He was happier and more himself among the friends he made at university than at any other period of his life. But not at the start: "For the first two years of his Oxford life Sebastian was slightly subdued. New College always had this Lenten atmosphere, unlike Christ Church or Trinity College, where there was the tinkling of glass every night. It was a temple of conventionality when Sebastian went up, dedicated to reading, drinking and chasing girls, none of which interested Sebastian greatly," as Eric Christiansen, then a fellow and now a don at New College, observed. "1964 was the crucial year of change, the year everyone wore jeans and bright colours" – till then they had worn cavalry twills and grey flannels. It was the year of the Beatles; and 1967 the year the Sexual Offences Act was passed, which made sex between consenting adult males legal.

Sebastian did not find the subject he had chosen, P.P.E., sympathetic: in the Prelims exam his Logic was pronounced "weak" by his tutor, "his essays have very limited depth and are too often marred by ugly English". He was rescued from these uncongenial studies by a clever, cultured don, Merlin Thomas, who took him on to read French. "I'm delighted to have him as a modern linguist – he seems very bright," he reported.

The two got on very well; Nick Montagu recalls, "Dr Thomas's magnum opus was compiling a dictionary of French slang to which Sebastian contributed. I remember him saying with glee '*Il y a du monde au balcon*', meaning that a woman is well-stacked." Sebastian was awarded an honorary exhibition in French, which brought "merely glory and the right to wear a more dignified gown". Merlin Thomas told him, "I recommended you to the College with a confidence that I know is not misplaced!"

Nicholas Montagu, Sebastian's contemporary at Rugby and at Oxford

As part of his degree course Sebastian went to France for a year, studying at the university of Clermont-Ferrand, and lodging in the town. Despite this and his natural aptitude for French he did not get a first but a second class degree in the summer of 1965. Afterwards, undecided as to what career to take up, he prolonged his Oxford life by studying for a higher degree. Merlin Thomas suggested the subject – the French historian Michelet, and his relation to the visual arts. Sebastian was interested in it, and he admired his distinguished supervisor, Professor Jean Seznec, who was attached to All Souls. While he was working on the thesis he also coached students successfully, which he enjoyed. But whatever his tutor might have thought, Sebastian was not cut out for academic life and the long years of solitary research necessary to get a thesis written and obtain a PhD.

What really enchanted him at Oxford was social life. He became, in the words of Eric Christiansen, "a memorable butterfly". The possibilities of society had begun to dawn on him in his final year as an undergraduate, when he lodged with one of the most snobbish landladies in Oxford, Mrs Hall, in Holywell. On her stairs she hung black-and-white photographs of members of the exclusive Bullingdon Club. As she prattled about her titled and monied young men, Sebastian began to realize that, while not actually joining them (he did not care for the sociability of clubs), he could expand his social horizons indefinitely – and this heady feeling stayed with him for the rest of his life.

He began to entertain when, as a recent graduate, he moved into a flat of his own in 1966. This was in Park Town, in an elegant, mid-nineteenth century house of pale grey stone opposite St Hugh's. Sebastian shared with a student of English, Nick Kennedy; he remembers that the garden flat was owned by a drunken clergyman who lived in the basement and used to beat on his ceiling with a stick when they made too much noise. In Sebastian's bed-sitter were the works of Michelet arrayed along one wall, his gramophone and record collection, of which he was proud – he had spent the whole of his first term's allowance on records – with a long table down the middle. Here he entertained: after the narrowness of Cheltenham and Rugby and the sobriety of his undergraduate years, now he enjoyed inviting whomever he pleased, and now he made lifelong friends.

He practised the sort of cooking he had admired in France, making no allowances for the restricted kitchen. Nick Kennedy remembers *blanquette de veau* with a delicate sauce, pigeons, and a Grand Marnier ice-cream which did not work: "He thought you could make it with equal proportions of Grand Marnier and cream, and what we got was Grand Marnier chilled soup."

At Nick Kennedy's twenty-first birthday party, which was held in the flat, Sebastian met Lady Selina Hastings, who was to become a close friend. She was reading English at St Hugh's. Selina was attractive, clever and, like Sebastian, generous and sociable. They got on well from the start.

"Sebastian had made Nick's birthday cake, which took him all day. It was chocolate and meringue and terribly, terribly rich, and he and I sat and talked about the cake all the time." They met the next day at lunch with Sir William and Lady Hayter – he was the Warden of New College. "He invited me back to finish up the cake and the left-overs from the party which I eagerly went to do, and then went back to my room and was frightfully sick all night. I told him and he said, 'My dear, we shall have to put you in training'; then we started going out to a lot of frightfully expensive restaurants.

"He talked about his work as though he loved it; he was very clever. He was then thinking of being an academic, he thought it would be right for him and he loved Oxford. There was something intellectually pure about academic life. He was very idealistic and thought it was a betrayal of standards to go out into the marketplace and how awful it was that people he knew had gone into journalism, for instance."

Selina Hastings, 1972. A close friend from Oxford days, she went on to become a distinguished biographer.

Sebastian and Selina spent a great deal of time together and he seemed more than a little in love with her. But, she says, "He was like a wonderful girlfriend. And I said, 'Yes, let's get married, ooh, yes, it's a lovely idea!' but we never got to the point of taking it very seriously.

"I think in his heart of hearts he terribly minded being homosexual because he loved women," and also, as he confessed in an (anonymous) magazine interview with Lynn Barber at the time, "One refuses to admit that one is going to be permanently queer, because one is so terrified of the prospects of growing up different from everyone else and not being able to have a family. It's the prospect of being an outcast … this is the kernel of the problem with queers – one feels one is not wanted by straight people." Because he found this realization "upsetting and traumatic", for two years he went to a psychoanalyst in London; he gave it up "because I ran out of things to say and it wasn't getting me anywhere".

This fear of rejection, or, in its more positive aspect, this need to be loved, was fundamental to Sebastian's character. It could never be satisfied. One manifestation of it was his endless social climbing – the need to be accepted by those whom he regarded as his superiors because they were socially superior – which was also done just for fun, as some people go mountain climbing.

Lynn Barber, 1973, journalist and author, who began a lifelong friendship with Sebastian at the University.

Then, as his close women friends testify, he loved their sex with a love none the less genuine for not having "this fund of goodwill that most straight men have towards ladies' bodies", as he inimitably expressed it to Lynn Barber. Wanting women to like him despite this made him court and flatter them the more. Certainly at Oxford he made many close women friends: Lavender Patton, whose son, Thomas, now a much-acclaimed composer, was Sebastian's godson; Lynn Barber; Marjorie Mayo; Dawn Ades (as she now is); Marina Warner, among undergraduates; Baillie Tolkien and Jude de Jonge, among dons' wives; and Iris Murdoch, Lady Hayter and Alexandra Trevor-Roper among the older generation.

Iris Murdoch, 1972. She and her husband, Professor John Bayley, were friends with Sebastian at Oxford. Sebastian and she saw each other regularly when he worked for her publisher, Chatto & Windus.

Life as a post-graduate student was definitely more fun for him than it had been as an undergraduate, especially in the mid-1960s. "I once dressed him up in my clothes as a dare," says Selina. "It was when everyone wore false hair and I had a lot of hair pieces and a nice little purple suit and a rather fetching purple velvet hat. I made him up, with a pair of false eyelashes. The only thing that gave it away was the size of his shoes. He couldn't wear my shoes, he wore his lace-ups, but at St Hugh's that was fine. I took him into formal Hall – that was the dare – and just as we sat down, and the Principal (Kathleen Kenyon), who was a terrific old lesbian, walked by on her way to high table Sebastian lost his nerve and ran out of the Hall and instead of running like a girl he ran with huge strides. I panicked too and ran after him. Nothing happened, but that weekend my parents were staying at Buscot with Gavin Faringdon[1]. When I went over there I told him and Patrick Kinross[2] the story of Sebastian and their eyes lit up like Catherine wheels and they said they'd like to meet him, so he went over and he took to it like a duck to water…"

Sebastian found the combination of the Bohemian and the aristocratic in Selina's world irresistible. As well as Selina herself, he loved her family, her mother, the distinguished writer Margaret Lane (whom he later recruited to write about animals and nature for Walker Books) and her father, the Earl of Huntingdon, the artist. He became a frequent visitor to their rooms in Albany, and their houses in Beaulieu, on the Solent, and in Tangier. As with the Davignons in Annecy, he embraced the entire family.

Holidays by the sea in North Africa were very different from those Sebastian had known on the damp English coast. "Sebastian was a huge success and my parents and I were very keen on him because most of the dinner parties there went on in French and his French was so good, but when he first went there he just didn't talk, for about the first week he just didn't talk at all," says Selina.

"I didn't realize, having been going out there

The Earl and Countess of Huntingdon: the artist Jack Hastings and the writer Margaret Lane, mid-1970s, parents of Selina Hastings, at home in Beaulieu, Hampshire

1 Gavin Henderson, the second Baron Faringdon – Labour peer, collector and former "bright young thing" with beautiful eighteenth-century house at Buscot in Berkshire 2 Patrick Balfour Kinross, the third Baron (1904-76) – Writer and journalist

for several years, how totally bizarre that life was, Barbara Hutton and David Edge and everyone and all the men in wild silk with emerald buttons and their faces painted and so on – he adored it! We used to go for picnics to these exotic pavilions on the Atlantic Coast and in the evening to a transvestite club which we thought was a great shriek. In the morning we would compete as to which of us could get up to the terrace where we had breakfast and tell my parents. I think it was a reaction away from what had gone on in his life before. It was a release – and *nobody said that this was disgraceful behaviour.*"

Back at Oxford, too, Sebastian found real happiness, always a rarity for him, through his friendships. These marked his tranformation into the sophisticated social being he remained for the rest of his life. From being a "temple of conventionality" New College had become much more permissive in the late 1960s: this was helped by the arrival of young dons, such as Eric Christiansen, Christopher Tolkien, who taught English, and Alex de Jonge, who taught French. Alex, with his Slav features, and Jude, his wife, who was reminiscent of Botticelli's "Primavera" gone astray, were compelling figures, as Eric Christiansen describes: "Along came the ecstatic vision of Alex and Jude de Jonge with their obsessive contempt for all forms of convention, and his passion for obscure French poets, notably one Lautreamont from the 1850s; Jude was blonde and glamorous with an unconcealed, frenzied hatred of Oxford. Both were young, vibrant, frequently intoxicated, and great

Sebastian at Christopher and Baillie Tolkien's wedding at Oxford

believers in the good things of life," not to mention, also, in their own superiority over the rest of mankind.

Jude de Jonge remembers seeing Sebastian for the first time: "Alex taught him and had often mentioned this bright pupil. We were driving down New College lane and Sebastian was bouncing – he didn't walk, he bounced – down the lane in his horn rims and his little sports jacket and his books under his arm." As he was to do at other times in his life, for example later on, with Nicola Bayley and John Hilton, Sebastian made himself part of the de Jonges' household. He felt at ease in their company, sure of their affection and happy in their house. Their mood fitted in with his; Alex recalls that "We were arrogant, impatient, very conscious of our own stylishness, and Seb picked up the lead from us and never put a foot wrong at a time when we loved to disapprove of those who failed to please us and meet our exalted standards. He was incredibly good at adapting to a house style, in this case ours, and later did it time and time again. Very, very smart and, I suspect, always looking for something elusive which he never quite found."

The de Jonges lived at White Hill Farm, Tackley, near Woodstock, just outside Oxford. "It was a large, grim stone farmhouse," remembers Eric Christiansen. "The interior had been cleaned and gutted ready to be redecorated, but much of it hadn't been, except for wall-to-wall carpets, oddly enough. It was spacious and welcoming with an immense ginger cat named Parker. Jude had a famously empty fridge, though they were hospitable with lunches and dinners going on a long time. Once those meals were over there was nothing left in the larder."

Jude recalls: "We were much freer then, we had no children and Sebastian had no regular job. He used to come for dinner and stay the night and in the morning he used to come into our room and clamber into bed while we decided what to do that day, and the laughter would start then." It would carry on throughout long lunches and dinners at Tackley or at Park Town. This was the only period of his life when Sebastian liked pop music, which he otherwise hated, and Ike and Tina Turner belting out "River Deep and Mountain High" was played over and over again.

His proximity to Sebastian served to emphasize to Alex that it was impossible to be really intimate with him: that he constructed intimacy consciously rather than feeling it spontaneously. He explains it thus: "Let us imagine, for the sake of argument, that this type of personality is, for whatever reason, incapable of experiencing emotion with the kind of ease and intensity that most people do, or think they do. As a result a whole order of intense and much talked of human experience is more or less denied them. Now this is not uncommon, but most people like that seek to compensate by channelling their energies in quite different directions, work or creative expression. Certainly, something of that clearly happened to Sebbie in his latter years, after I knew him. But his case was much more interesting. He was highly intelligent and certainly aware that a large part of the spectrum of human experience was closed off to him. But, and here is the trick, rather than dismiss it as unimportant, he was intelligent enough to realize that it was perhaps supremely important, both as a source of happiness and as the force that drove most other people.

"As a result he sought to use intelligence, inference and intuition to make an artificial construct of it, one which enabled him to mime emotion, behave as if he, too, had such feelings. The only thing was, that whenever he talked of feeling, or allowed his construct to shape his behaviour, you had the uncanny feeling that something was ever so slightly wrong. It was like hearing a colour blind person discussing a painting. The sense of form and tone were there all right, but you always had the feeling that their account missed some fundamental aspect that you took for granted."

This central trait in Sebastian's character, so well-defined here, was sensed by many of his friends, but often masked by his natural affection and generosity. Alex de Jonge goes on to say: "It may be this absence that made him so good at friendships, and so bad at anything stronger. But, and this is the point, it drastically alters one's sense of his sexuality. He may have gravitated to his own sex because he used to be so nail-bitingly shy, or else because sex with men did not necessarily involve an emotional component, could be reduced to mere sensation more readily. But be that as it may, I have the sense that Sebbie was sexually active out of an almost *a priori* feeling that this is what people do, not because he was 'naturally' like that.

"It was all a kind of cultural construct, behaviour adopted from some sense of the obligation to be, or appear to be, like others, for reasons ranging from camouflage to a common sense view that that was the best way to pursue happiness; pretend you are not colour blind and one day it may feel as if you can see it all.

Oxford's golden couple, Alex and Jude de Jonge, 1969

"This is the theory I use to explain that strange sense one had about him that, in some fundamental way, he was out of touch with others, while trying to sustain the illusion that this was not the case by the way he used to nod and mouth his agreements, those slightly drawn out nasally drawled 'Yesses'."

35

This aspect of Sebastian's very complicated personality, which was to become more marked as he grew older, accounts perhaps for the loneliness so many people felt in him: but was it loneliness, or was it just a preference for his own company? Maurice Sendak was to notice later that however well one got on with him, there came a moment when he "put the shutters up" on any further intimacy.

Meanwhile, at Oxford, he continued to see as many friends as possible. Entertaining was a natural medium for him; he cooked everything himself, of course, and the more elaborate the better. Eric Christiansen remembers the occasion when Sebastian gave a dinner party for himself and Alex de Jonge to meet his parents. "I could just see his father and his moustache at the far end of the table: all went fairly well, but the trouble was that neither Alex nor I could stand up, having drunk too much. A bowl of trifle was passing in front of me and I lost my balance and my head dropped into it: it was felt that neither of us had upheld the honour of the university."

On another occasion Sebastian invited his parents to meet his supervisor, Jean Seznec, who greeted them by saying enthusiastically, "Your son is the best cook in Oxford", praise which did not go down well with Richard Walker, who thought his son was at Oxford to learn, not to cook.

Sometimes Sebastian drove out of Oxford to eat in restaurants in the country. On one occasion he and Nick Kennedy were stopped by the police as they drove back. Sebastian beamed his wide-eyed, innocent stare on the policeman but he blinked so hard in his attempt to look innocent that his contact lenses came out and he had to drive home to Park Town very slowly indeed.

To Sebastian, who had always thrown himself into acting and dressing up, a highlight of these post-graduate years was the production of Marlowe's *Dr Faustus*, with Elizabeth Taylor

Sebastian filming
Dr Faustus *in Rome*
with Richard Burton,
1966

and Richard Burton. The play was directed by the charming and civilized professor of English at Merton College, Nevill Coghill, for whose sake Taylor and Burton had agreed to act without a fee in the undergraduate production, since Coghill had introduced Burton to acting when he was briefly an undergraduate during the war. Now, twenty years later, he had come back to repay what he felt to be his debt of gratitude.

The Burtons appealed to all Sebastian's love of star-gazing. He had the small part of the Horse-Courser and, after rehearsals started at the beginning of 1966, he was an instant fan of Liz Taylor – "I can see down Liz's dress, enormous melons, my dear," he told Nick Kennedy back at the flat, and he regaled Selina Hastings with imitations of Liz putting on her third pair of false eyelashes. When the play opened at the Oxford Playhouse in February 1966 it was "terribly amateurish with Elizabeth Taylor seriously overweight coming on in a toga and a cloud of dry ice. We thought it was wonderful," says Selina. "It was a university production, no one thought of anything except spotting Taylor and Burton; to pretend that anyone was interested in Marlowe would be misleading."

Following the stage production, Burton and Taylor decided that there should be a film of *Dr Faustus*, and with a generosity lavish even by their standard they took the forty-eight undergraduates in the cast to Rome, where the movie was shot. Sebastian loved that summer of 1966: he started off in the Peloponnese with Alex and Jude sightseeing and "draping himself round the cafés" as Jude described it; then on to Rome and the pleasures of making the film, shopping, strolling and carousing. The film opened to less than rapturous reviews the following year. After *The Times* had panned it Sebastian wrote to the editor to acknowledge the generosity of Burton and Taylor in giving their support to the film as well as the play.

While he was in Rome, Sebastian bought some slim-fitting

suits with colourful linings, and silk shirts to go with them, from Brioni on the via Barberini. He was immensely proud of them and they did look marvellous on him. But, explained his flat-mate Nick Kennedy, his pleasure in wearing them was short-lived, for the flat was robbed. "I came back one day and Sebastian was leaping up and down outside saying, 'They've stolen five silk shirts! They've stolen five silk shirts!' My signet ring and a pair of desert boots had also gone, and the detective came by and said, 'Well, if we see someone wearing five silk shirts and a signet ring and a pair of desert boots we'll pull them in.'"

They were never traced but it is probable that this was the doing of one of Sebastian's casual lovers.

Nick Kennedy found there was a slightly maniacal quality about his way of life: "He spent quite a lot of time in town on his own but it was something he didn't talk about. He never brought boys back. He played it by the book. He knew that it was not something that was part of the scene then. Things changed radically over the next ten years."

That promiscuity was an integral part of Sebastian's life he explained in the anonymous interview with Lynn Barber: when she asked, "Why are homosexuals so promiscuous? Is it because it's so difficult to have a happy emotional relationship?" instead of exploding, as he would have done ten years later, Sebastian replied: "Yes, it is. So one doesn't bother. Also sex is easier to get without either party expecting emotional involvement. But the disadvantage of not being able to have a family, not being able to be married stably (because homosexual marriages are notoriously unstable) is fundamental, connected with the fact that one is not the same as other people. It is so fundamental that one must shut one's eyes to it and try not to let it perniciously influence one in other ways. This is why queers are so bitchy normally, you see. They're getting their own back the whole time."

This feeling of apartness emphasized here was, as we have seen, reinforced by Sebastian's nature. Perhaps this is one reason why, all his life, Sebastian set so much store by friendships, such as the one that grew up between himself and Lynn Barber and her husband, David Cardiff. They reckoned that Sebastian got more from friendship than most people and felt secure now with his circle of friends around him.

He may have been happy at Oxford, but academic life was not fulfilling, and he decided the time had come to abandon it. It was not that he was pulled urgently towards another vocation, nor suddenly eager to get out into the marketplace. He had found his work, at any rate at the beginning, intellectually stimulating: the file of closely written notes, which is all that remains of his thesis, testify to his interest both in Michelet the historian and in the visual arts. One of the problems, common to many PhD students, particularly at Oxford, was that the amount of supervision he got was inadequate to spur him on to do the solitary and detailed work. Sebastian's supervisor, Jean Seznec, though clever and cultivated, was remote. Apart from the odd "Bon Courage" from him, Sebastian seemed to be battling on unaided; after two years' research he was no nearer the end and, after all, what would he do with his thesis? The original goal of becoming an academic seemed less and less appealing. Intellectually, Sebastian had gained a lot from his seven years at Oxford, besides finding a unique happiness and

David Cardiff, 1972, media historian, artist and husband of Lynn Barber

lasting friendships; what he had not discovered, however, was where his talents really lay — although at least he now was confident that he had some talent. The single-mindedness which was to characterize his career as a publisher later on was nowhere in evidence.

His ideas ranged from going into publishing to becoming a chef. He sometimes cooked for parties for such friends as Hugh and Alexandra Trevor-Roper, which he enjoyed. But a chef was not then considered a career, although Sebastian, with his knowledge of French, love of food and wine, and gregarious temperament, might have made an excellent one. His father certainly did not approve.

Sir William Hayter, the Warden of New College, who, with his wife, Iris, had become among Sebastian's most sympathetic older friends, arranged an interview for Sebastian to enter the security branch of the Foreign Office. At the interview he was asked, "Have you anything else to tell us?" "Yes, I'm homosexual." "That doesn't matter as long as you can keep it under control." To which Sebastian replied, "I have no desire whatever to keep it under control." And that was the end of his diplomatic career.

So what was on offer now, with fluent French, seven years of Oxford behind him, and no especial inclinations?

"I think I shall drift into industry," he had said when Sir William Hayter asked him that question.

"Oh, you must do better than that!" Sir William replied, to Sebastian's father's chagrin. He therefore decided that if his son wanted to "drift into" the family engineering business, Walker Crosweller, he had better start elsewhere, at the bottom, and get some proper training. "I was sceptical about whether Sebastian would like the rough and tumble of industry."

Sebastian finally found a place as a trainee in group management in a light engineering firm, B. Elliott, in Acton, West London, earning £19. 4s 6d a week. He rented a room for £7 a week, in a flat belonging to a journalist friend, Virginia Ironside.

London Life

Virginia's flat was on the two top floors of a stuccoed early-Victorian house in Royal Crescent, on the edge of Holland Park. Her mother, Janey, was the first Professor of Fashion at the Royal College of Art. Her father, Christopher, was an artist and designer. The decoration of the flat was spare and well thought out, with white walls, white shutters instead of curtains, polished wooden floors and original pictures, in particular by Virginia's uncle, the artist Robin Ironside.

To Virginia, Sebastian was the perfect lodger – not least for his ability to rescue her sauces: "I was always going to him wailing, 'My béarnaise has curdled!' and he'd say, 'Don't worry, darling,' and put it right." She remembers how he did everything in great style, he was an early "foodie", going to the market to buy fresh ingredients, though what he did with them was not always a success. "He had dinner parties non-stop, a tight little circle of Oxford friends." Holland Park is conveniently situated near the end of the A40, the main route from Oxford, thus providing a continuous link. As there was no dining-room in the flat, Virginia and Sebastian would put up a long trestle table in the kitchen on which to eat his creations, which were ever more rich and elaborate.

Many of his weekends were spent at Crichel, in Dorset, staying with his close friend Patrick Trevor-Roper, the eminent eye surgeon, whom he had met in Oxford with his brother, the historian, Hugh.

Patrick shared a country house with the music critic Desmond Shawe-Taylor and the literary critic Raymond Mortimer. It was a remarkable nest of bachelors, hospitable – their cocktails of gin and Dubonnet sent guests spinning merrily back through the Dorset countryside – and cultivated. The walls in the drawing-room were papered with a brown watered silk pattern and there were many paintings by artists who were friends, such as Duncan Grant and Edward le Bas. Desmond Shawe-Taylor had an extensive music collection here, and he often used to take Sebastian to concerts in London. During the weekends there would be visits to such neighbours as Lord and Lady David Cecil at Cranborne or Cecil Beaton at Rockbourne, and there were often distinguished guests staying, such as the composer Lennox Berkeley and his wife, Freda. She was to become one of Sebastian's closest friends over the years: limitlessly sympathetic, motherly and amused, with a musical, rather cooing, voice, she was, above all, tolerant – nothing ever shocked her, an essential quality for a confidante of Sebastian's. He often visited the house in Little

Virginia Ironside, 1973. Virginia found Sebastian the perfect lodger when he shared her flat in Holland Park.

Venice where she and Lennox lived with their three sons, and he would talk on the telephone to her by the hour. Sebastian always enjoyed mixing the generations at his dinner parties, and his tongue-tied young guests would often find themselves confronted by a formidable array of distinguished older people.

His social life was in great contrast to his working days at the factory. Early every morning he would set out for Acton. "He was very impressed by the other workers who had 'levvers', as he called them, and motor-bikes, so he went off and bought himself a set of 'levvers' and a bike which caused him great difficulty in starting. He was very proud of both of these, but shortly afterwards he broke down and arrived back very late at night, sweating in his 'levvers', having had to push his bike all the way from Acton. He was exhausted and furious!" Virginia Ironside remembers.

Sebastian got on well with the other workers despite their teasing him on account of his posh accent and strange name and the fact that the other apprentices, being school leavers, were mostly ten years younger than him. That Christmas he took Virginia, well-known for her long legs, to the works dance, telling her to wear her shortest mini-skirt. Generally speaking, he enjoyed his work making machine tools in, as he put it, "an amazing factory" with "butch machines". As a trainee he worked on the shop floor, fitting, turning, milling and grinding with spells in various departments, stores and accounts. B. Elliott was part of a large group owned

A mini-skirted Virginia Ironside accompanying Sebastian to the Christmas party at B. Elliott's light engineering factory, Acton, 1969

by a clever businessman, Jack Frye, who was both successful and innovative. Whether his success meant anything to this particular apprentice on the shop floor in Acton is not known, but it cannot have been a bad thing for him to be a part, however small, of a highly successful commercial enterprise.

In December 1968, a few days before his twenty-sixth birthday, Sebastian's mother killed herself. She had been mentally unbalanced for years, made unhappy and highly emotional, partly through her own imaginings, partly through real depression. Although her years of instability had perhaps prepared her family for her final unhappy end, and despite having had, latterly, a troubled relationship with her as her irrational demands made her increasingly difficult to deal with, Sebastian was nevertheless profoundly shaken by his mother's suicide and it left him emotionally vulnerable.

After a year in the Acton factory Sebastian left to join the office of Max Fordham, mechanical engineers in Camden Town. The outcome of his two years' training in engineering was meant to be his joining the family firm, Walker Crosweller. That was the plan; what scuppered it was his change of heart about going into industry in general and the family firm in particular. It had taken him until now, his twenty-eighth year, to question closely whether or not it was really his destiny, as he had been led to believe by his grandfather. There was, too, the presentiment that working for his father would be no more fun than it had been for his own father to work for *his* father.

A job as "a special assignment representative" at Walker Crosweller starting at a salary of £1,500 a year was created for him by his father. Sebastian never took it up; on the day he was supposed to start, October 1, 1970, he wrote to his father that it might be better for him to gain a qualification at a business school; that ultimately he wanted to be considered a potential director. "In the short term I do feel that my graduate status is greater than the context of Walker Crosweller is prepared to admit, that my three post-graduate years were not wasted, and that my two years in engineering so far amount to more than a demonstration that I can hold a job down. In the long term, I feel that I can only accept a job where my employer explicitly

envisages me as an eventual director; if I come short along the line I expect to be sacked: my eventual position is to be gauged, as is the speed with which I attain it, exclusively on my ability. At no point will I expect my inherited wealth or my name to push me onto, or push me out of, a boardroom."

Sebastian and his father, 1972. Despite differences in outlook, they had a great mutual respect.

Sebastian felt that his father did not appreciate him, either for his intellect or for his adaptability in moving from academic life to the lowest rung of the engineering ladder. Far from welcoming his only son unequivocally into the family business, as his grandfather would have wished, Sebastian thought, his father assessed his potential rather too dispassionately, as parents tend to do, especially fathers of their sons. Sebastian regarded his stipulation that he should eventually be made a director of Walker Crosweller as perfectly reasonable; his father did not. Considering that at the eleventh hour his son had failed to take up the job he had especially created for him, it was with restraint that he wrote to him on October 6, 1970, asking "What sort of life do you want? There is a deal of difference between the world of the publishers and the engineers... Decisions on your career must be made by you and you alone ... and on this point you can – and I say this with complete sincerity – ignore my feelings... I applaud your ambition to make your own career..."

This letter disproves what Sebastian was inclined to put about in later years: that he had not joined the family firm because his father "had not wanted him to"; but while it is true that his father tended to be dismissive of his work so far, he had all the same gone to the lengths of creating an opening for him in the family firm. The fact is that Sebastian was probably more aware than he realized of the pitfalls of father and son working in such close proximity and that he was better off starting up his own enterprise in an area he found more sympathetic than engineering. Ironically he was to use what he saw as his father's lack of faith in him to spur himself on to ever greater achievements when he eventually set up on his own: it was almost as if he needed that spur to goad him.

Meanwhile he was twenty-eight and aware of the need for a "proper job". He had gone down an academic path and a technical path, and both had come to nothing. As certain as he was that these were not right for him, he knew also that he had to find something he believed he could do. His more perceptive friends recognized that he should become a businessman of some sort: his analytical mind and combativeness combined with his charm would find it enormously invigorating. "But the other half of him wants to be able to say that he does something superficially fascinating. So he's persuading himself he should be an art critic," wrote Virginia Ironside's husband, Robin Grove-White, in his diary. "It's a matter of showing him how to discover that gratifying his mind will be more rewarding than gratifying his snobbery in ten years' time, because the former in fact will govern the latter. It must be very hard for him … but he has a very tough mind and is aware of the alternative."

The idea of becoming an art critic was short-lived. Sebastian now inclined towards publishing, not because he was especially drawn to it but because he was not drawn to anything else in particular. He went to see everyone who would give him an interview or who could offer him work in publishing. He told Virginia, "They're all so relieved to find I'm not some intellectual dilettante wanting to write poetry. When I say I can read a balance sheet they squeal with delight." (Balance and music sheets remained his favourite reading from then on.) So the autumn of 1970 was spent in looking for work which was congenial, until eventually he found a way into publishing.

Sebastian with Rosalind Toynbee, the eldest of the bevy of Toynbee sisters

By this time Sebastian had bought a house of his own, 29 St Paul's Place in Islington, a terraced house, which cost £13,400, raised by a loan from his father and a mortgage. It was tall and narrow with steep, creaking stairs. In the basement, originally the coal cellar, was the dining-room. There were bedrooms on the ground floor for lodgers; a double drawing-room on the first floor and Sebastian's bedroom upstairs. Unlike later on, he enjoyed surrounding himself with lodgers. Now they included two of the many Toynbee sisters, Clare and Rosalind, with whom he had been at Oxford; they brought with them a

cat from their home in Yorkshire. Sebastian tolerated rather than liked this animal. "So the cat led rather a precarious existence, it got good food, but it was not much liked," said Eric Christiansen, another of his lodgers, who was in London to do research.

Clare Toynbee, as an undergraduate, bicycling in Oxford, 1969

Life at St Paul's Place was not very different from life in Oxford. It was comfortable, casual, but with a certain formality imposed by Sebastian's entertaining. Sebastian bought furniture, none very grand, and rugs at auction. Eric's contribution was a model of the Taj Mahal in a glass case which was prominently displayed in the drawing-room. The walls were mostly painted plain white and there was no attempt at elaborate decoration beyond four white plaster palm tree lights, said to have been Syrie Maugham's, in the corners of the basement dining-room and a pair of silvered wrought-iron gates which separated the dining-room from the kitchen adjoining it. A devoted cleaning lady, Mrs Smythe, came in for 6/- an hour. She also "did" for neighbours, who included the author Richard Adams, then writing his cult novel about rabbits, *Watership Down,* while working as a civil servant in a Whitehall warren.

"Sebastian ran an orderly house," Eric Christiansen remembers. "We all had our duties and Mrs Smythe had hers. I think he would have liked the cat more if it had been less independent, and had helped with the dusting. When it was party-time the tradesmen rolled up with boxes of wine and gilt chairs and the more bizarre forms of confectionery on time and at the right house; Sebby knew them all too well for mistakes. One day he stood by the caramel thermometer for seven hours to make sure the stuff was all right on the night. He had his own heavy linen for the tables and the sort of knife-handles you could stun a man with. It was not a grand place at all, but he put on a grand show.

"That time-expired coal cellar was never an entirely convincing dining-room; the stairs rocked and rolled up past the lodgers' rooms to the drawing-room and that was an Islington folk-museum of kitsch, art deco and Beidermeier. You could be very comfortable there, with a coal-fire, and the gramophone and the drinks, and the television. That was how we spent un-social evenings.

"Food did what he ordered. Big red pieces of beef graduated from superior butchers and submitted to the massage of mustard, pepper and clove, and wallowed in their own juices and the bath of Burgundy. Salmon flopped the length of a table, steaming, out of the silver baths which had crowded the kitchen, and pyramids of profiteroles were in fact more like spires. Nobody could stand the Eggs Huntingdon, true; but the rest of it was so dreadfully good that it was, or seemed, impossible to live up to.

"Sebastian couldn't, anyway. By the time the *Timbale Lucullus* and the 'boring old roast beef' were on the table, he was too tired to talk and too tired to eat...

"So the guests did most of the talking. Out of all that cataract of words I can only fish up two dispiriting conversations which, at the time, I had hoped to forget. One when X told me the plot of a serious novel she was writing, and I had to bite my tongue to avoid laughing, and the blood came, and spoilt the roast lamb. Another when Plante, the American (the writer David Plante), gave a sort of speech about artistic integrity in a muffled voice that ruled out any sort of reply from me at all. Why these? Perhaps they were the only intellectually ambitious responses to Seb's cooking that year; at least it proves that we didn't spend all our time shouting 'Come off it, Ducky' and getting drunk.

"Some of those people were Leftish: Marina (Warner), for one. I noticed that Sebastian was quite immune from that sort of weakness, and in fact disliked it as much or more than I did. He believed in capitalism and property and all that; he never spoke a word on politics, but there were signs that he knew who was minister for what, which was more than Clare or me. Perhaps he was waiting for Thatcher, but not in matters of rent: he undercharged and subsidized our inefficiency, and shielded us from the market in a way she would not have liked. In fact St Paul's Place was a sort of sanctuary for a number of *cigales* beginning to feel the cold of the market (a pity it had to end)."

Sebastian presided over the large polished round table on a Freemason's chair, or at least so he described it, with arms and a tall straight back with some kind of mystic symbol inlaid in it. He was given to wearing caftans, bought on his jaunts to Morocco, and there he sat, berobed on his great chair, like some snub-nosed potentate dispensing a great deal of wine and extremely rich food.

He liked meat that had been well-hung, for longer than most butchers were used to doing, and in fact he frequently hung his beef too long, so that it smelt off while it cooked and tasted slightly high. An historic duck pâté is recalled, with only some exaggeration, by Virginia Ironside: "He'd been out to Bermondsey market at seven in the morning and bought a lot of delicious fresh ingredients, let's say fresh shrimps, avocados, chicken livers. Put with them some best brandy, home-made yoghurt, truffles, pistachio nuts. He then puts them all in the liquidizer, with a duck that he's taken out of its skin and boned, adds an egg, two bottles of brandy and mayonnaise and cooks for three hours, liquidizes again with shrimp essence and uses as stuffing for the duck skin which is laboriously sewn up with a great upholstery needle, then presented, surrounded by watercress. It looks a lot like an American football with legs and I'm afraid tastes a bit like an old one. However, everyone clamoured for second helps (except for me, who'd wisely only taken a piece cut off the narrow end) with cries of 'Sebby! How delicious! What a menu.' Whereupon Marina (Warner) asked where the word 'menu' came from and Alex (de Jonge) promptly told her."

Sebastian himself was capable of sending up his love of rich food and did so in an article he wrote for the Private Cooks page of *Harper's/Queen* magazine in 1973: "In a utopian world, everyone would want, every night, my ideal menu, ice-cream, followed by ice-cream, followed by ice-cream. However, it is important for the host to avoid that hush which falls at the end of an over-rich meal. Cream, oil and butter are the killers, and if, like me, you never tire of all three, everyone else will feel sick very quickly, unless you either control their portions of each course, or safeguard their livers by your choice of menu.

"A bachelor who cooks is someone who lives with a slice of domesticity missing: there are just certain areas of household management that make my skin prickle with panic, and one of them is everyday cooking. If I am on my own I want to eat fried eggs out of the pan, standing at the stove. However, ask five, seven or nine friends to dinner, and then I want a soft musical progression of flavours and sensations, snatches of appreciative compliment, and with quiet excitement, to present and preside over the perfect meal."

Although written tongue in cheek, this does show the perfectionism Sebastian applied to everything he did: no amount of planning, no attention to detail, no effort was too great in pursuit of perfection, whether in business or music, in publishing or pleasure.

He went on, "I always use English sea salt in preference to any other, because I find it is the best (I like to think, fancifully perhaps, that it contains a soupçon of seaweed)." His insistence on fresh ingredients lasted all his life: "I had a treat this summer when rung up by my greengrocer at seven a.m. from Covent Garden to be told that wild strawberries were cheap today. He bought me ten pounds. I puréed the whole fruit, and using less cream than usual, but orange juice and Cointreau, made one of my best ice-creams ever."

Apart from this fancy food (he once described his cooking as "formidably indigestible"), Sebastian also liked plain home cooking, "nursery food" like his beloved Mel's shortbread, for instance, stewed fruit, home-made jams, mashed potato and swede when cooked with enough attention to keep in all the flavour.

Sebastian had the social confidence to invite whomever he liked to dinner: there was still the core of

Oxford cronies, and among older friends, he became very fond of Sir Alfred and Lady Beit, who invited him to stay at their eighteenth-century jewel of a house, Russborough, in Ireland, and with whom he often went to the opera. Eric Christiansen's view is that Sebastian "had only made one momentous decision about himself, perhaps at Rugby: 'I must not be shy'. Shyness and shame were then defenestrated, if he had ever known them; and this, I think, gave him a head start in the social stakes, since most of the other runners, even in the 1960s and '70s, were handicapped with various weights of guilt, embarrassment and the dross of self-criticism... Most of us (no names) couldn't really enter a roomful of people, let alone some kind of personal transaction, unless we were plastered.

"Sebastian didn't seem to need that... His art was to move among us with our varieties of dingy reticence and self-control, and publish his own joys and sorrows without fear."

Certainly, "dingy reticence" was never part of Sebastian's makeup: whatever was on his mind he shared liberally with those around him. At this time the family circle was enriched by our father's second marriage, to the journalist Sidney Gordon, whom we ourselves had known all our lives – she is, in fact, my godmother. Attractive and affectionate, she treated us,

Sebastian's stepmother, Sidney, in 1972, shortly after her marriage to Richard Walker. She was a good friend to both of her stepchildren.

her stepchildren, as if we were her own, always welcoming and hospitable to us and our friends.

Another home from home, where Sebastian was always welcome, was Lennox and Freda Berkeley's house. It provided what Sebastian liked best – music (Lennox composed at home),

good food (Freda is a generous cook) and Society (Lady Diana Cooper lived next door). Amongst their friends, Sebastian often met the formidable Norah Smallwood of Chatto & Windus. Now that he had decided upon a career in publishing, he continued to make it his business to meet as many publishers as he could.

Lennox and Freda Berkeley at home in Warwick Avenue, Little Venice

"Seduced by the Likes of Sebastian"

Sebastian's search for employment, something with intellectual respectability and commercial prospects, ended in 1970, when he landed a job, not on the literary side, but as a European sales representative for Jonathan Cape. He got this job not through connections, but on merit, and by wanting it badly enough to persuade sceptical directors that he could do it. He was interviewed by Norman Askew, who had been sales director at Cape for the last fifteen years. "A very, very sensible, staid chap who wouldn't have been seduced by the likes of Sebastian," according to Graham C. Greene, who was then managing director of Jonathan Cape and joint chairman of the Chatto and Windus, Bodley Head and Jonathan Cape Group, three publishers which had joined together for organizational purposes. Greene, who was to become a good friend of Sebastian's, genially admits that at the time he thought the idea of giving the job to Sebastian was "a very silly one". Where he would normally have nodded it through, now he said to Norman, "'You're crazy, this man won't last six months in the job. It's really a waste of our time and money.'

"Norman saw Sebastian again and he promised that he would stay five years. I said, 'That promise isn't worth anything. If he gives notice you can't keep him' and Norman said, 'You've always said we should have younger, better-educated, brighter reps and now the first time I produce someone along these lines you say I can't have him!' And I said, 'Yes, but I have talked to Sebastian Walker and it is self-evident to me that his ambitions are far greater than to be a rep, and he has a social life that will preoccupy him and he'll never do this job properly.'

Watercolour of Chatto & Windus' offices, by John Ward RA

"Norman still fought, which wasn't his nature at all and so Sebastian came and did the job to the day practically that he'd promised – and did the job remarkably well."

Jonathan Cape was a well-established publishing house founded fifty years previously; it had a good general list and high-quality children's fiction, with Arthur Ransome and Hugh Lofting among its authors. Its founder, Jonathan Cape, who had died in 1960, made a point of crossing to America to buy outstanding titles which were little known in England and to sell English ones, a transatlantic market which Sebastian was also to cultivate when he founded his own publishing house.

For Sebastian the five years, to 1975, which he spent as European Sales Representative were a good, tough training. He started on the road in January 1971 with a punishing itinerary from Paris to

Brussels on to Hamburg, and all over Germany. It was a demanding and lonely life, in the car and visiting bookshops and publishers, persuading them, on the evidence of dust jackets or proof copies, or just an outline, to place orders. Sebastian worked hard at it, learning the market from within the marketplace. He spent the evenings in hotels or opera houses. As he drove he listened to operas on tape. "He'd come back and say: 'The Ring took me all the way to Italy and back,'" remembers Clare Toynbee, "and he'd go to La Scala and listen to whatever was being performed."

He managed not to let this arduous new regime interfere with his social life too much: Graham C. Greene remembers meeting him on the steps of Albany – "where one never usually met one's reps as one came home from the theatre!"

At the same time as he was selling books, he gave up reading them. Once on the plane back from the Frankfurt Book Fair a colleague complained of having nothing to read. Sebastian got up and disappeared into the lavatory where he tore the book he had with him, *Majesty*, by Robert Lacey, into two and handed him half, saying, "Well, I couldn't have done it with everyone looking – I'd have been lynched!"

Selina Hastings recalls being on holiday with him in Morocco at this time. "Sebastian and my mother and I did a trip to the Sahara; he had a novel he had to read by George Mackay Brown about medieval peasants on Orkney [*Magnus*]. We were staying in a wonderful hotel in Taroundannt, a French-Moorish hotel on the edge of the Sahara with banana plants and every luxury. He tried reading for a quarter of an hour and then with a heavy sigh said, 'You know, the awful thing is I just don't like reading' – and he put the book down and I don't think he ever read again" – well, almost never. But, unusually for junior employees in publishing, he did read *The Financial Times*, taking a keen interest in "bottom lines".

Every year he went to the Frankfurt Book Fair and thoroughly enjoyed the buzz of selling and meeting foreign contacts. "He walked quickly round it, he was very positive, loved meeting people, everything was a-buzz and it was infectious. That was the only time I ever enjoyed the fair," recalls John Charlton, then an editorial director at Chatto & Windus. "He made many contacts for us which later on he could use on his own account."

He also took the trouble to cultivate some key figures in the Cape-Chatto-Bodley Head group, who would be important in his life later on, notably the head of Chatto, Norah Smallwood.

As a result, according to his friend Eric Christiansen, he "seemed to be changing from a butterfly into a caterpillar; at least he used to wear a businessman's suit and apply himself seriously to self-improving schemes, such as learning German and Italian, and playing the piano. The caftan was now confined to the bedroom, or possibly lost. The brown velvet trouser suit was not seen at all. He had stopped shrieking as often as he used to, possibly as a result of the jaw operation." This was an operation to correct Sebastian's overhanging bite (a feature of the family teeth). It was a horrific procedure whereby his jaw was broken and then wired together so that for weeks he was in pain and for months could eat only puréed food. It also changed the shape of his face.

"He led a treble life," continued Eric. "One part was at the office, and travelling to book fairs when he was the rising young man. The second part was with his friends, when he still played the entertainer, made mischief and drew out confidences.

"The third was the homosexual part, which he threw himself into as seriously as into the book trade. There were probably other parts of him as well. The opera-going was almost a life in itself, and so was the cooking, although it was for the benefit of his friends. As I never saw him at the office, or in the erotic quarters of North London, I only knew one third of him, at the most." That was probably as much as any of us ever knew of him.

In 1973 Sebastian left the house in St Paul's Place and its jolly population of lodgers for a dignified abode in nearby Canonbury. It was a commodious Victorian family house, semi-detached with a walled garden at the back where he lovingly tended,

among other things, a marijuana plant. It would be proffered round of an evening and had about as much kick as a cup of tea.

Sebastian with Donald Richards in the garden of the house they shared in Alwyne Place, Canonbury, 1975

He set up house here in Alwyne Place with Donald Richards, an Australian in his twenties. Donald had only recently come to England in order to finish his history thesis, which, like Sebastian's, was eventually abandoned. A lithe young man, with "college boy" good looks, thick brown hair and "come-hither" eyes, he was clever, though unoriginal, given to mouthing Sebastian's views. He was kindhearted, but indiscreet about the attentions of other men (which seemed to be numerous). Able and hard-working, he shared Sebastian's passion for the opera and for entertaining. For the first, and last, time in his life,

Sebastian essayed a domestic relationship. Rather unconvincing as it sometimes seemed from the outside, he, at least for the time being, believed in it. Maybe since I, and numerous of his friends, got married and started having families at this time, it was another example of his feeling that one "ought" to have a relationship now. For whatever reason, Sebastian was anxious that his friends and family should like Donald and accept them as a couple. Any backsliding was pounced upon, usually exaggerated and never forgiven.

The house was decorated not in the cheerfully random fashion of St Paul's Place but in a rather ponderous manner reminiscent of the furnishing department of a large store in the late 1950s. To save time, and because he felt that this large house needed living up to, Sebastian used an interior decorator from Cheltenham who made heavy damask curtains for the drawing-room with tie-backs of velvet grapes and introduced conversation pieces such as a glass-topped coffee table upheld by gilt sphinxes. There were pale green blinds.

"They treated the light with great suspicion," said Eric Christiansen. The drawing-room walls were ragged in a similar green paint; it gave onto the dining-room, "silent, grave, expensive rooms". There were one or two pieces of furniture which had belonged to Sebastian's grandfather, such as a sideboard by Voysey and a settle by Mackintosh, but no allowances were made for their particular style. Pictures ranged from two oils by his friend David Scott which hung in the drawing-room to a blown-up photograph of Sebastian floating naked on a lilo which hung above the bath flanked by another of glamorous young footballers in the changing room. There were more bedrooms on the top floor, where Walker Books would eventually get started.

Sebastian had begun to have piano lessons with Joyce Hedges, a teacher recommended by Freda Berkeley. Under her sympathetic instruction he rediscovered the pleasure he had found in the piano, which he had been taught throughout his schooldays, but had only played intermittently since. From now on it was to have an ever larger part in his life, but at this moment he was content to have a lesson once a week and to practise regularly. He played on his mother's Bechstein baby grand over which was draped a silver-embroidered cloth.

In 1975, virtually five years to the day after he had joined Jonathan Cape, he left. He had enjoyed his time there, but he was ambitious, and his success in sales had made him conscious of his worth; he wanted promotion and none was offered. He decided to broaden his scope and, from the up-market group of Jonathan Cape, Chatto & Bodley Head he moved to the very different firm of Marshall Cavendish.

Marshall Cavendish originally published partworks on practical subjects like crafts, and their books were spin-offs from those. They had little in common with the traditional publishers Sebastian had been working for: "If you said the word 'author' they looked slightly worried and if you said the word 'royalty' they were completely speechless," says Nick Kennedy, Sebastian's old flatmate, who had joined the firm straight from Oxford. Their offices were in St Martin's Lane in the centre of London.

Sebastian was their salesman for Europe and also started their children's list, and so continued to deal with European publishers. "He was one of the best communicators of ideas I've ever worked with," says Nick Kennedy. "We had one French colleague, Pierre Zech, who said, 'I don't like seeing Sebastian because I always end up buying books I don't want' (a view that was to be expressed frequently in years to come).

"He was totally bewitched by Sebastian because once we were having a meeting to discuss a book and halfway through Sebastian said, 'I have to leave now'.

"'But why?' asked Pierre.

"'You're coming to dinner with me and I have to go and buy the wild strawberries and then I've got a piano lesson to do my Schoenberg,' said Sebastian."

This mingling of business and private life was always a feature of his career, one which he carried off with panache.

Perhaps the most important thing his two years at Marshall Cavendish showed him was the possibilities of publishing for a mass international market – such co-editions were to be the basis of the early success of Walker Books. "Sebastian was the first to do these properly and successfully," says Judy Burdsall, who was at Marshall Cavendish with him and went on to join the fledgling Walker Books. "Publishers covered England and America, but he got many more editions going" and this accustomed him to large print runs – the average at Marshall Cavendish was sixty to seventy thousand of such illustrated books as *The Small Garden* by John Brookes.

Sebastian had other insights into publishing two years later when he left Marshall Cavendish to rejoin his old employers, this time as a director of Chatto & Windus, a traditional, closely knit firm; their premises were in a tall, narrow eighteenth-century house in William IV Street. It was still headed by the doyenne of British publishers, Norah Smallwood. In a life like Sebastian's, studded with formidable females, Norah Smallwood was surely among the most redoutable. Now nearing seventy, she had joined Chatto & Windus forty years before as a secretary: her obituary speaks of "the awesome energy and determination that took her from a secretary's desk to the chairmanship of Chatto & Windus". Even though she was afflicted by arthritis those qualities never let up. Sebastian had made it his business to get on with her when he had first worked for the publishing group in 1970. It was not always easy; she liked her own way; she treated all employees as if they were her assistants, whatever their rank; she was cheeseparing (Sebastian's salary as a director was only £6,000) whereas Sebastian was by nature generous and also believed that money talked if you wanted something, or wanted someone to do something. Having said that, there were many qualities to admire in Norah and much to learn from her. She cared for her authors above all. "Norah's authors stood at the centre of her world: she dedicated herself completely to them… Iris Murdoch's pre-eminent position in English fiction was the abiding pride and pleasure of Norah's publishing life," wrote her obituarist. She also cared very much what books looked like.

Although Sebastian's working relationship with Norah was not always harmonious and he fretted at the tight rein she kept him on, nevertheless the discipline, the professionalism, the respect for authors, the small firm with a recognizable identity, all this he understood.

Sebastian was in charge of children's books and he also initiated an illustrated adult book which was to prove highly successful. The idea for *The Englishwoman's Garden* came to him after spending a weekend in the country with James and Alvilde Lees-Milne and observing the energy and creativity that his hostess lavished on her garden. The ensuing book, with many contributors and photographs of all of their gardens, was a great success worldwide and led to a series of books along the same lines, from *The Englishwoman's Kitchen* to *The Englishman's Dog*. But by the time even the first of these was out Sebastian had left.

Although at Chatto he had what he wanted, a directorship of an interesting publishing house whose chairman must surely retire soon, he was no longer interested in being part of a company. At thirty-five he wanted to go it alone: he had worked out the figures, mainly on the backs of envelopes, and knew that what he wanted to do was feasible, that the market was there, a global market for selling children's books which were better produced and illustrated than any others, in co-editions of tens of thousands; now he was impatient to get out there and sell them.

Starting Up, 1978

To raise a loan for his new company, Sebastian approached his father's bank, William's and Glyn's in Pall Mall. He arranged to meet his father beforehand, at the Reform Club, that venerable Victorian Renaissance building in Pall Mall. Men were not allowed into it without a tie, so Sebastian, in his open-necked shirt, fell at the first hurdle. The porter, having registered his disapproval at his tie-lessness, produced the necessary item, and so he could enter and go over the figures again with his father.

As the new venture would be expected to pay its way in three to five years, the bank would want to see financial forecasts on a monthly basis for three years. Sebastian had prepared an initial cash flow for four books, followed by another series of four, all to be pre-sold as international co-editions. For the first four projects his forecast was a gross income of £279,100 and an expenditure of £130,400. He sought a loan of £20,000.

That fine May morning in 1978, father and son (Sebastian still wearing the borrowed tie) crossed Pall Mall to the bank; like the Reform Club it also had family connections: for seventy years his father and grandfather had banked there.

The manager questioned Sebastian closely on his figures and the assumptions on which they were based: did they, for instance, take into account rising costs, particularly of the best quality colour printing? Sebastian's confidence that he could launch this new venture single-handed clearly impressed him. He agreed to lend him the money, providing he had guarantees from both father and son: so the loan was doubly secured, at 3% over a base rate of 9% (which rose to 12% over the year). The shares in the family business were not involved in the transaction except in so far as Sebastian could not have given his guarantee without his holding shares.

Gradually in the late summer, Sebastian Walker Associates came into being. Who were the associates? In recruiting the first of these Sebastian made one of the most inspired choices of his career.

Amelia Edwards was an American of thirty-eight, whose work as a designer he already admired: "On our first meeting at Marshall Cavendish, Sebastian asked whether I had designed a particular book. When I said that I had, he said, 'I could have sold it over and over again, it's brilliant!' and I thought 'Really' – excuse the word – 'this is bullshit, but I like it!'

"I became unhappy at Marshall Cavendish and that May, 1978, I decided to resign, but I'll never understand how, the very next day at 8.30 a.m., I got a call from Sebastian asking me to help him find designers: 'Well, you've found one right here'. 'YIPPEE!' he said and we met later in the day and he helped me to resign." Helping people he wanted to work for him to resign from their current employment was never a problem for Sebastian.

Amelia went to work for him a few months later at £7,000 a year, half what she reckoned she would have earned as a freelance designer. "I felt this was going to be fun, more fun than anything else, and I had nothing to lose, no mortgage and no babies, so I could afford to do it. But it wasn't long before he started rewarding me; and when someone came and asked me to do some consulting, he said, 'I'll pay you not to do that.' That was the first time I felt his need for loyalty. I said, 'You don't have to do that, there really isn't time, I can't do it.' Later on, he was obsessive about loyalty."

Initially, Sebastian's team were all women: he believed that there were a lot of talented, under-used women in British publishing and he was always happy to employ them in the highest positions, reckoning that they were as capable of taking responsibility as men and less encumbered with their egos. In October, in a seedy pub at the bottom of the Tottenham Court Road, an editor was recruited, who, like Amelia, was to stay the course. Wendy Boase, an Anglo-Australian, had been the children's book editor at Marshall Cavendish.

"I came to meet Amelia and Sebastian at this squalid pub with stained red plush upholstery. I thought the whole project was terribly exciting and I said I would give in my notice and join them."

By the end of the year Sebastian had installed his small team of four, two designers and two editors, at the top of his house in Alwyne Place. Already there was a family atmosphere, which was to be a characteristic of the fully fledged company: the sound of Sebastian's piano playing would float up the stairs; Donald would sometimes cook for them all – chilli con carne was his speciality. Sebastian was still titivating his house, his latest project being an elaborate back garden which was not so much a garden as a gravelly space with slender trees; he thought it the last word in landscaping and ignored those who said it was like a municipal park.

They all worked very hard; office furniture was bought second-hand and extra tables and chairs commandeered from around the house. Wendy contributed her own portable typewriter. To begin with, the books they were working on were deliberately unadventurous: four gardening books and four books about pets, all non-fiction for eight- to twelve-year-olds:

Amelia Edwards, art editor, Sebastian's first recruit to his new publishing house, May 1978. She soon became "the heart of Walker Books".

"Sebastian said we had to start with something safe, that you know there is a market for, and then we could do more adventurous things. He knew he could sell this sort of non-fiction and we knew we could produce it because we had done it at Marshall Cavendish," said Wendy. She herself started working on four books on pets, *Know Your Pets*. "From the beginning Sebastian trusted us to get on with producing the books without interfering. One day we had our first visit from a foreign publisher, Philippe Schuwer, who saw work in progress and he was terribly rude about it. We felt wounded to the quick. We didn't cry in front of him, we waited until he had left.

"It was a new venture and we so loved what we were doing, but it was a valuable lesson because it made us revise our ideas. Sebastian didn't come into the room, he let Philippe come in and talk to us about the books on his own and he stayed away. He gave us that kind of liberty right from the beginning which is the thing I remember most about his style. He gave you the sense that he employed you because you were good and he trusted you to get on. His trust was his sign of affection."

By the spring of 1980, when the first titles were ready for publication, the fledgling company was installed in proper offices off the Tottenham Court Road. They had moved the previous year. Wendy and Amelia, in order to economize, organized the move themselves with a couple of helpers and two very reluctant husbands who kept reminding them that it was Cup Final day and they would much rather have been at home watching the football.

The new offices were not prepossessing. Sebastian never believed in fancy addresses. They were on the top floor of Hanway House, an erstwhile sweatshop: "Where a hundred Cypriot seamstresses had worked away we painted the brick walls white and moved in, still with the same second-hand office furniture," said Sebastian in an early interview.

To get to it you went past an Indian restaurant and up and up an iron fire escape through a cloud of spicy curry smells, sometimes bypassing the curries themselves, put out to cool. There was a less picturesque hazard when the Council started using pesticides to kill the rats attracted to the dustbins: the staircase was littered with their corpses. "They crawled up towards our premises to die," said Sebastian. "I felt sorry for them."

He was delighted with the new offices: from the flat roof there was a wonderful aerial vista of the bustle of Tottenham Court Road and Oxford Street and the secret alleyways around them. It was a far cry from the established publishers in Bloomsbury just across the road. "American and European publishers staying at the Connaught love coming up the fire escape to see us. They're tired of seeing the same old books as they have done for the last fifteen years in grand offices in Bloomsbury," said Sebastian firmly. Every morning he bicycled down from North London, an improbable Irish tweed fishing hat crammed down on his curly head, and his papers in a bag like a school satchel slung over his shoulder.

He shared the offices with Peter Inskip, the architect who later designed his house, who remembers that Sebastian's working hours were then, as always, very much of his own making. "He might come in late because of his piano playing at home. There would be quite a lot of going off to the gym, long telephone calls to Freda Berkeley, Lady Caroline Somerset, Lady Beit, the social and the business calls all mixed up, and he would often go home early for his social life," or for more piano, interspersed with business calls.

These early days were not without their crises which required all Sebastian's decisiveness. The printers, a firm near Bath, nearly caused the whole enterprise to be still-born. Their first results were not good enough, the colours not true. "When we were unhappy with the print we were getting," remembers Amelia Edwards, "Sebastian said, 'Come on, Amelia, pack up your art work, we're going to Italy!'

"I said, 'You're going to pull out of all the promises you made to those printers? I mean, I'm coming!' So we went, and he completely charmed the printers in Bologna into doing new proofs for us, and of course they were spectacular."

The delay would have scuppered two large orders from German and Swedish publishers had not Sebastian visited both and, by showing them the original artwork, reminded them of the difference between it and the first printed result which would be improved upon – as it duly was. "If you're determined enough as a young business you overcome such crises, no matter what. If you take 'No' for an answer anywhere along the line you shouldn't be starting up on your own anyway," was Sebastian's crisp conclusion to the crisis which nearly wrecked his venture.

"Printing prices are now more competitive and quality is more secure in Italy than in England. Of *course* I would prefer an English printer. Apart from anything else it would be more convenient. Unfortunately, they're just not good enough for the high standard of colour printing which I need to sell my books worldwide."

Sebastian saw his company relying on foreign co-editions: England would

Wendy Boase, editor, one of the initial team to start work in Sebastian's top floor spare bedroom

be only a small part, fifteen per cent of his market. One of his earliest deals was to go to Sweden with the first eight titles, the quartets on gardening for children and on pets, and to sell twenty thousand of each to Birgitta O'Nils at ICA, a large publishing house which had never published any children's titles before, in a royalty-inclusive deal.

"It was an experiment for them," recalls Wendy Boase, "and that's what very largely financed Walker Books for the following year. The books didn't sell and we didn't sell another thing to ICA but at Frankfurt, after Sebastian's death, Birgitta came onto our stand and said that she was bereft; that's extraordinary for a publisher who overbought on books which they never managed to sell more than ten years before, but Sebastian had kept up with her over the years."

Once the books were at "sample stage", with the

artwork and the dummy ready, and they had been pre-sold worldwide, Sebastian said, "I felt able to approach an established British publishing house to expand on the home front." The firm he went to was Methuen, whose backlist reads like every well-read child's bookshelf: *Babar, Tin-Tin*, Dick Bruna's books, *Wind in the Willows,* and that ursine superstar, *Winnie the Pooh.* Walker Books, as it was now named, and Methuen became partners, with Walker included on Methuen's list for promotion and sales in all English language markets except the United States. The young company did not have the resources to do these for itself, and this link with Methuen gave it excellent promotion, selling and distribution, while the older company had an injection of new titles and new ideas. As far as the foreign market was concerned Walker Books was autonomous.

"To start on your own, you don't in fact need a great deal of money. What you do need are books that are original and well-produced. Non-fiction for older children requires a great deal of effort: the editor and the designer are as important as the author," said Sebastian. Eight out of the seventeen titles he first published were non-fiction, the rest were picture books, including four written by myself, beautifully illustrated by Christina Gascoigne, whose first books they also were. The history of their publication highlights the difference between Sebastian's publishing approach and the established one.

I had sent my quartet of seasonal stories to Tom Maschler at Jonathan Cape some while before, at Sebastian's suggestion. Maschler had liked them and was looking for an illustrator, and looking … and looking. *Eighteen months* passed without my hearing any more from him, or any money changing hands. When Sebastian started, he asked to see my stories again; within days I had a cheque for the option of publishing them, and he had found Christina Gascoigne to do the enchanting pictures for them.

The star of his first list, and of many lists to come, was Helen

Oxenbury, whose recruitment was a coup for Sebastian. He had met Helen and her husband, John Burningham, the writer and illustrator, when he was with Jonathan Cape, John's publisher, and they had become good friends. Sebastian knew that Helen's illustrations were what he wanted for his list; never one for the oblique approach, he drove up to her house in Hampstead and put the proposition to her over a cup of tea.

The illustrator Helen Oxenbury, Sebastian's first prize in 1978

"He arrived at the house one day, late in 1978, when I was about nine months pregnant, to ask me to illustrate something for his new list," remembers Helen. "I thought, what a jolly idea! I'd liked him from the first time we'd met and I thought it would be nice to start afresh because you do become taken for granted when you've been around some time.

"We talked about what I should do; it was the time of pop-up books, novelty books. I'd had a *Heads, Bodies and Legs* book as a child, by Trier, a Czech illustrator, I think, and I'd loved it." They agreed on that, and as for terms, "I said that all I could offer her as an advance at that time was a measly five hundred pounds," said Sebastian, "to which she replied very sweetly, 'Oh, don't bother to give me any money till you've earned a bit' – which of course one never forgets. I kept terribly cool, but I was so excited that when I drove off I backed my car into a lamp-post! Anyway, I never had the 'Oxenbury bump' taken out because it just seemed such good luck really."

Soon afterwards Helen had her baby, Emily, and Sebastian came to the hospital every day to visit. "I thought, how nice, he's come to see the baby; in fact, he would spend two seconds on the baby and then, 'Now, Helen, when do you think you could get started?'"

Helen Oxenbury and John Burningham. Helen's Heads, Bodies and Legs, *(below) was followed by her supremely successful baby board books, created for her daughter Emily.*

Within a few weeks Helen was working on a trio of *Heads, Bodies and Legs* books while Emily was sleeping in her cradle: *Crazy Creatures, Assorted Animals* and *Puzzle People*, each £1.95, proved to be terrific sellers. Helen brought to what was a somewhat downmarket idea a sense of fun and of vulgarity which especially appealed to children. The production of the books was first-class, with excellent colour reproduction on good quality paper.

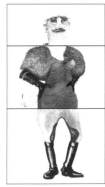

With or without Sebastian's blandishments, Helen enjoyed working for Walker Books: "It was such fun. I loved Hanway House, even slipping down those stairs on fish heads. Sebastian would have to sweep all those old bones away when an important American publisher came. Once inside the premises there were lines of windows, beautifully proportioned" – a legacy from its days as a sweatshop.

If it had been unusual for an illustrator of her calibre to embark on *Heads, Bodies and Legs,* it was unheard of to go in for her next venture – baby board books. These were normally cutesy productions of puppies and kittens, very downmarket. Helen Oxenbury made them witty and appealing, to babies and to their parents; on their second list, in 1981, they were Walker Books' biggest sellers all over the world. With them they discovered the vast market for children below reading age. Part of their success was that they were based on a real-life baby, Emily Burningham. When Emily was about six months old, Helen and John were searching for something to entertain her: "She had this awful eczema, and left to herself would scratch herself raw, so we tried to keep her amused. We went and looked for little board books for her, because she could recognize images in catalogues and that sort of thing." Not finding anything, Helen started using Emily herself as the model for the plump, bald baby who is the beguiling central character of her board books.

Selling these books for babies worldwide carried Walker Books out of debt and into profit. This is reflected in their figures: in the first ten months, to June 1979, before trading really got under way, there was a deficit of £19,868, not including any salary for Sebastian, nor bank interest of £866. Sebastian's father, who continued to advise him, recalls that "a number of orders had been obtained from publishers abroad and advances on these provided an income, but prudent accounting dictated that these advances should not be regarded as sales until the orders were actually delivered and invoiced.

"In the second year, to June 30, 1980 (that is, the first year of publication), sales were £187,043. There was a loss of £13,047, not including any salary for Sebastian. Bank interest was reduced to £15. But in the third year, to the end of June 1981 (after two years of publication), sales were up to £895,951. There was a profit of £57,892, sufficient to pay for the losses of the first two years and to pay off the bank. There was enough left for Sebastian to draw a modest salary. So Walker Books was through the first three critical years.

"By 1982 sales were £1,161,656, of which £907,350 were exported, continuing a remarkable record of exports – £102,811 in 1980 and £688,003 in 1981 – remarkable for a company so small and so young." Richard Walker concluded that, "This outstanding growth, from zero to over one million pounds in four years, owed nothing to fashionable trends, or unexpected or inflationary rises in value. These were years of recession. Sebastian's original concept of the market for children's books was sound: he supplied a product which was original and excellently designed. He kept costs, particularly overheads, low and so was able to sell his books at prices the customer would pay. His sales policy and methods were imaginative and unencumbered by the tradition and myths of the publishing trade."

Sebastian with Helen Oxenbury and Emily Burningham in later years

"Having a Marvellous Party"

Sebastian ran his infant company with his own heady blend of seduction and coercion, on a basis of tireless energy and enthusiasm. The top floor of Hanway House was a-buzz; visitors who bypassed the cats and toiled up the steep iron staircase found a staff who seemed unexpectedly young. They were not, particularly, but their eagerness to succeed and the feeling they gave of playing rather than working, "of having a marvellous party and being paid for doing what they were best at", as one visitor put it, contributed to that impression.

From the beginning Sebastian was determined that Walker Books should be "author-led". Helen Oxenbury observes that "with many publishers you become a bit of a nuisance when you come in to the office, but Walker Books was completely the opposite. Didn't someone in a publishers once say, 'We ought to have a special room set aside for authors and illustrators because they do get under your feet when they come in'? You never felt that with Walker Books. You couldn't not like Amelia. Then again, most publishers take you for granted after a few years and stop getting enthusiastic about your work."

Sebastian was always enthusiastic, kept up with his authors on the telephone, and invited them to dinner and to concerts. But he was a businessman too, and, like any other successful business, Walker Books was also market-led. Sebastian referred to "marketing the package", and getting "the formula" right so often that he could have been selling clothes or package holidays, and he kept his eye steadily on "the bottom line". In 1981 he acquired another key member of the team, David Ford, an American, who came initially as part-time bookkeeper.

David Ford, who, within a short time, became the backbone of Walker Books

"My part-time working was shortlived because Sebastian couldn't bear anyone to be part-time, to share anyone with someone else. I remember him saying to me, when I was going to research another book with James Lees-Milne, 'What do I have to do to prevent your doing it?' and I didn't understand what he was saying. I was then paid £5,000 full-time. Then, as he did with everybody, I got rather large raises, rather quickly, not exorbitant sums, but I remember not liking it. It was as if he was paying more and more and asking more. It was very successful, wasn't it? It was what he did with authors and illustrators too. It eventually has the effect of making you think that you can do better: 'He thinks I'm good enough for this, therefore maybe I am.' The effect it has on you is to make you wonder 'How am I going to live up to all these expectations?', with the result that you work all the time feeling insecure, that you can't possibly measure up!"

To David Ford, as to many other people, Walker Books was a two-man band – Sebastian and Amelia Edwards. "She was every bit as responsible for the success of Walker Books as he was. She treated artists with respect and affection." This was a novelty. Normally designers took an illustrator's work and made it into a book without consulting the artist about it at all. Amelia made illustrators feel as important as any other constituent of a book and that their work deserved the best-looking result possible.

"If he was the brains, she was the heart of Walker Books," says David Ford. "The extreme loyalty of authors and illustrators was due as much to her as to pecuniary rewards. She gives the feeling that nothing is too much trouble. She was the kind, healing Mother Earth. He was Daddy and she was Mummy!"

The search was on for new authors and illustrators. Sebastian's approach was direct. One of his early lists might have included a life of Hitler had not Hugh Trevor-Roper, Regius Professor of History at Oxford, replied, on November 24, 1978, to his request: "You must forgive me if I do not accept your kind suggestion of writing a biography of Hitler for children. I do not think that Hitler is a suitable subject for children at all, and I don't think I can catch the right idiom anyway."

Other overtures were more fruitful, for instance, to the beautiful and talented Nicola Bayley. She looks like a heroine from a fairytale, with her black tresses cascading down her back, large, expressive eyes and gentle smile. When Sebastian met her she was an unhappy heroine, in the grip of a powerful editor at Jonathan Cape, Tom Maschler, who tied her to an inexorable round of illustrating large-format books despite her protestations that what she wanted to do was what she was best at, illustrating on a *small* scale. She had successfully illustrated seven books for Cape, who had recruited her straight from the Royal College of Art. Maschler looked after her – he had declared "I'll be your publisher, your agent *and your friend*" when they had concluded their first deal – but he would not allow her the freedom she craved to illustrate tiny books. "He said people wanted value for money and these wouldn't sell because they wouldn't think they were getting it," Nicola recalls.

Her first impression of Sebastian was a physical one: she was taking him a book from a mutual American friend and climbed the steep iron staircase of Hanway House and there he was to greet her at the top, "broad shoulders leading straight up into his neck, like the neck of a bottle, like an Elizabeth Frink sculpture – and those devilish eyes!"

Across the office Amelia watched them: "I could feel his magnetism," she says. "He was sitting at his desk and Nicola was getting closer and going back, getting closer and going back, and I thought 'We've got her!'"

Sebastian wooed Nicola through his habitual channels, music and mutual friends. She and her husband, the barrister John Hilton, were going to hear Montserrat Caballé with a mutual friend who invited Sebastian to come too: "Sebastian asked me if I was happy. I said that as a matter of fact I was not, I had got into a rut, and what I was happiest doing was teeny-weeny things. 'But, darling, of *course* you can do tiny books!' he said.

Right: Nicola Bayley's illustrations from Copycats *(top), 1984, and* The Mousehole Cat *(centre and bottom), 1990*

Nicola and her son, Felix, Sebastian's godson,1988

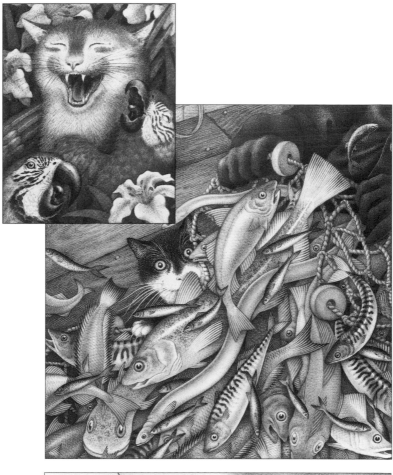

"'But I can't do books for anyone else.' 'You don't have to do books – you can do *friezes*.'

"My first roughs were in the shape of friezes. It didn't take me long with Sebastian to realize that I didn't want to go back. At Walker Books they were more interested and interesting. With Cape I would be given my text and go away and do my work and hand it back – a letter-box system. There was no involving *me*. At Walker Books everyone was always so *pleased* with what you'd done, they concentrated on *you*, and weren't thinking about some jumbo-author who'd just written a Booker Prize winner. You got the feeling Cape were publishing books, and then there were the children's books.

"And then nobody could resist Amelia; and Sebastian had the ability to make you feel completely wonderful and the best person around and he couldn't wait to see your next book."

As was often the case with his authors and illustrators Sebastian became great friends with Nicola and John and with their small son, Felix. He frequently visited their colourful and welcoming house in Stockwell. The first time he went there he admired the pictures in the sitting-room, many of which are of girls: "very fuckable", he pronounced, to which John replied mildly that "he hadn't thought of them in those terms."

Copycats, published in 1984, were the first little books Nicola produced for him.

Nicola Bayley and her husband, John Hilton, Q.C., 1981. Nicola and Sebastian (right) at Mousehole to promote The Mousehole Cat, *1990*

Sebastian's "poaching", as other publishers regarded it, was generally disapproved of in the business. His direct approach, cheque book in hand, to authors or artists who had been nurtured by another publisher, was regarded as sharp practice which bypassed the conventions. A hint in their direction was considered enough; but Sebastian was in too much of a hurry for hints. He regarded his method as fair game if authors or artists were dissatisfied with their publishers, either because they were not

given enough money or enough attention. They did not *have* to change after all, but they might actually prefer to join a small, specialist company which published only children's books and was therefore likely to concentrate more on them.

Besides wooing talent, selling books worldwide was what Sebastian was best at, whether abroad, in the office, or at book fairs. The most agreeable of the fairs, held every spring at Bologna, was mounted just outside that handsome city in tubular hangars. Unlike some fairs, Frankfurt for instance, Bologna is a civilized occasion, small enough to walk round comfortably and with plenty of places to sit down outside and eat *gelati*.

At first Walker Books had too few titles to fill their stand at Bologna so they would dispose of some of the shelves to make their display look decently crowded.

"In the old days, at Marshall Cavendish, Bologna was very much a jolly where you met your friends and had drinks with them, and much drinking went on and you would leave the stand unmanned while you went off to have lunch and in the evening go out to discos. It was *not* like that with Walker Books. You were there *to sell books*," says Judy Burdsall.

Judy Burdsall, head of production, had worked with Sebastian at Marshall Cavendish.

One of Sebastian's talents was being able to sell in four languages. He could switch easily, and persuasively, from English to French, Italian or German. Another was a technique he perfected, and passed on to his staff, of presenting the idea for a book, or a series, in no more than one minute. He even managed to do this with a book called *The Story of Life*, one of his ideas for a type of encyclopedia to explain the world to eight- to-twelve-year-olds. David Lloyd, who joined Walker Books as an editor in 1981, remembers: "Off we went to Bologna to sell the co-edition. In those early days the editor presented the book to foreign publishers. I'd not been to Bologna before and I would probably be stopped after seven or eight minutes into *The Story of Life*. Sebastian explained that the whole point of the exercise was to present it very fast and if they said no, accept it and move on... He would present it in about a minute; what he said made little sense but it sounded quite convincing. It didn't matter what was actually said as long as it sounded right."

Frequently Sebastian took authors and artists to Bologna Book Fair just for the trip to Italy in springtime. This also made them feel very much a part of the Walker Books "family". As such an author, I could only watch, in awe, the arcane performance of selling in several languages as Sebastian kept appointments without pause, with the same level of enthusiasm at the end of the day as at the beginning.

When the fair was over he enjoyed staying with his friends, the painters Matthew and Maro Spender, in their Tuscan farm, where white doves circled and there was always plenty of home-made wine; there he relaxed following a ninety-hour week of selling, selling, selling, looking unaccustomedly pale in a dressing-gown, speechless but happy, like an actor after a tumultuously successful performance.

David Lloyd joined the team as an editor in 1981, when he was introduced to Sebastian's fast-selling techniques.

In the course of selling Sebastian was frequently over-ambitious about such details as delivery dates, and his desk would be peppered with furious little notes from Judy Burdsall: "SEBBY! Why did you promise that we would deliver by...?" Usually, though, the little notes were written by Sebastian and left on his employees' desks. He would come in on Sundays and leave his "droppings", as they were nicknamed, for Mondays.

His hours in the office continued to be unpredictable – perhaps deliberately so – and he would often slip out unnoticed to play the piano which he had had hoisted up and installed in the stationery shed on the roof outside the office. He would tell Judy Burdsall he was "just going out for a quick plink-plonk" and if he was needed she would go out and retrieve him from among the piles of stationery. He would not let anyone hear him, saying that he was not good enough for an audience; he preferred to play alone in his shed on a rooftop off the Tottenham Court Road.

Maro Spender. After the hurly-burly of the Bologna children's book fair, Sebastian recuperated at Matthew and Maro Spender's beautiful farmhouse in Tuscany.

Within a comparatively short space of time Sebastian had assembled at Hanway House the small group which formed the core of his company: David Ford, who became Managing Director; two editors, Wendy Boase and David Lloyd; Judy Burdsall, who was Production Manager and, of course, Amelia Edwards. He regarded them as his family, and demanded absolute loyalty from them. He did all he could to bind those he trusted, loved or needed to him by flattery, financial reward or emotional manipulation.

For a man as complicated as he was, some of his reactions were childishly straightforward, particularly towards people leaving: he hated it. Partings were always charged with emotion whether they were amicable or not; they brought out all his fears of being rejected, that he might be abandoned. In the case of David Ford, who soon became his right-hand man, this was true even of his going on holiday.

Once, when David went on a fortnight's working trip to America, followed by a fortnight with his family, he returned to Walker Books to find Sebastian distraught at what he regarded as his defection.

"It's unbelievably emotional as a company and I think that's its strength and also one of its weaknesses. It's a real cauldron. It's not a job, is it, it's a great deal more than that, and I think he purposely created it to be that," says David Ford; or perhaps because to Sebastian it was so much more than a job he expected it to be the same for other people. "He was constantly testing and manipulating. His insecurity was at the centre of everything" – the more so as the business became increasingly successful and Sebastian himself increasingly isolated.

An exuberant Sebastian on top of his world of books, drawn by Chris Riddell, 1987

The Wizard

From its first 17 titles in 1980, Walker Books expanded to 66 in 1983 and 141 in 1987. Sebastian began to realize that he should be independent from Methuen. The arrangement with them had been more than fruitful.

"He made that brilliant deal, and how on earth he was able to make it I cannot imagine," says David Ford. "The thing that he stood fast about was that at the end of five years the rights would revert to him, that was the crucial thing and they were very foolish to agree to it. They gave too much away. So that when Walker Books separated from them, by March 1987, within a very short time the Oxenbury board books, for instance, became Walker Books' property. Sebastian had retained the rights to sell them to the book clubs and anywhere else, and he did so in quantities. Methuen had put in all the hard work establishing them and yet didn't get the long-term benefits." The profits to be gained from the humble board book when drawn and designed well and marketed exhaustively had not been apparent to them, as they had not been to any other British publisher.

"Hanging on to the paperback rights of all his books was another far-sighted deal. Where he learned all that who knows, but, boy!"

Success did not lead to more glamorous offices for Walker Books. In 1984 the expanding company moved from its original unprepossessing office to still less elegant premises further north up the Tottenham Court Road, in Drummond Street, near Euston Station. This had been a garment warehouse and the cage-like lift, big enough to carry racks of clothes, took up most of the stairwell. The stairs themselves were narrow and uninviting. Through grimy windows could be seen similarly ill-favoured buildings and a car-park. There was little charm in the immediate surroundings which consisted of slab-like modern buildings or older ones forlornly awaiting demolition by the hands of the philistine Camden Council. Still, in contrast to Hanway House, there was at least an inside staircase, no smell of curry and cats and, for the first time, the company's own switchboard.

Choosing downbeat premises "was to do with being able to look people like Helen Oxenbury in the face and not feel guilty; wading through deep pile carpets in the office would not have enabled him to do that," says David Ford. "What would authors think if they came into smart offices furnished with their money?" Besides, an office with a post-modern facade, plate-glass doors, pretentious pieces of sculpture and a nail-varnished receptionist smacked of a Corporation, which Sebastian loathed: to be a tycoon, yes, corporate man, never. He was his own man, and he had his own methods of establishing Walker Books' identity as the accountants at one of the early audits learnt when they told him, "You've got to cut down on frivolities." Sebastian asked what they meant by frivolities.

"Well, these fresh flowers," they said.

"I'll cut down on accountants before I cut down on fresh flowers," he replied crisply. There were always bunches of flowers in the offices of Walker Books, properly chosen, not just impersonal carnations.

A news-sheet, "Walker Weekly Whispers", circulated the office with such items as "There is a new art director at X publishers called John Grandits. He actually sounds as though he possesses a brain. At last!"; or a recipe for Boston Baked Beans, from David Ford; or news that Amelia Edwards would be spending a week in North Yorkshire with the author William Mayne: "She will be staying in a post office, where from six p.m. every night, she will sit alone reading her book. During the day, she and William are going to lay out *The Blemyah Stories* on his word processor – which will also produce the final typesetting to be used in the book. This leads the art department to the possibility of getting a word processor, with which they can do all their typesetting"; this was in 1986.

Sebastian started office lunches in the new premises, cooked in a little kitchen and served in a dining-room, free to all staff and their visitors. They originated because there were no decent restaurants in the area and they continued because they were pleasant and economical for the employees, who also spent less time away from their desks, more time discussing work with their colleagues – and kept them out of the pub. It was an excellent way to entertain artists and authors, making them feel involved with the company, part of "the family".

This unusual set-up, in such off-putting premises, came as a surprise, as the author and illustrator Jill Murphy discovered when she first went there. Sebastian had approached her with his usual directness: having been given her telephone number by a mutual friend he rang her with the opening words: "I'm Sebastian Walker, a successful children's book publisher."

Jill Murphy asked him to send her his latest catalogue. This greatly impressed her. "For one thing it was better laid out and printed than most publishers' actual children's books and for another it contained all the people I admired – such as Jan Ormerod, Shirley Hughes, Colin McNaughton and Helen Craig.

"I went to have lunch with them when I was next in London and the contrast between the other publishers I went to see and Walker Books was just extraordinary. It was like the Tardis; you went up these strange stairs and opened this rather grim door and the place was filled with light and flowers and people who were pleased to see you … and the lunch, one realizes now it was structured, you were fêted. It was just a delight. I remember thinking, 'If they're like that all the time…' which they were. That's the other thing, they never changed, they haven't changed to this day in their attitude. People generally change once they've got you, whether it's a man or a publisher!"

Jill Murphy was happy to begin work for Walker in 1986, and her books about elephants, the Large family, became best sellers.

For Walker Books, Jill Murphy wrote and illustrated the best-sellers *Five Minutes' Peace, All in One Piece, A Piece of Cake* and *A Quiet Night In*. Like other Walker Books' artists and authors, she was delighted to be encouraged to work in the office if she wanted. "I met the other authors. I had never met other authors in my life!"

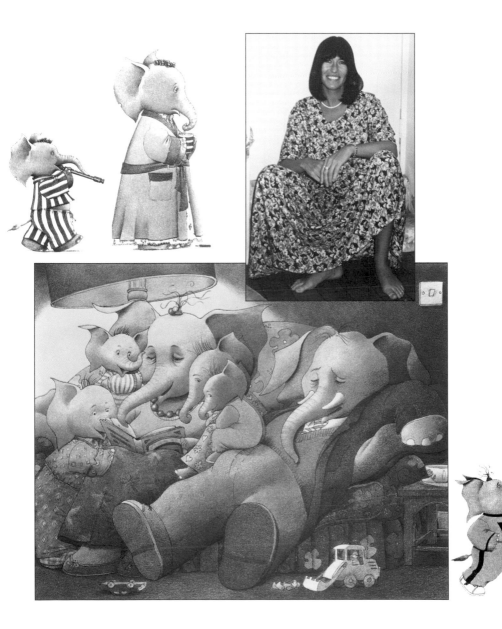

Experienced authors and first-time ones agreed with her. Sebastian's brother-in-law, the historian Hugh Cecil, was presented with a sumptuous box of watercolours, like a child getting the best Christmas present it had ever dreamt of, and given a contract to illustrate stories about teddy bears, which he and I had written and laid out. Sebastian was overflowing with enthusiasm for them: "It will be in a tradition of distinguished academics writing and drawing for children – C.S. Lewis and Tolkien."

"The atmosphere of the company," wrote Hugh Cecil, "even by the time it quadrupled in size, was quite unlike that of most publishing houses. There was excitement, new ideas perpetually being tossed about,

a feeling of joint endeavour… One could hear talk ranging from whether it would be better to have the latest co-edition printed in Singapore or Italy to whether a bear in an illustration should be allowed to have a cigarette hanging out of its mouth (it was, but in a later edition it was expunged)…

"Sometimes there was a feeling that we were in a children's book – Sebby himself seeming like some miracle-working magician and some of the editors

Hugh Cecil, Sebastian's brother-in-law, whose illustrations for Teddy Tales (1980) *were in part inspired by the editorial staff of* Walker Books looking as if they were dressed for the circus, propelling themselves about the floor of the office on their swivel-seated chairs."

Mostly the magician's spells worked and the room would be illuminated by his smile; but sometimes they went wrong and then, watch out! There were flops, titles which sold badly, and even, once, a whole series. These were the Zebra Books, intended to compete with Ladybird Books, the small format, highly coloured books which sold everywhere from petrol stations to corner shops. Zebra Books were similarly highly coloured, with a larger than usual typeface, and included non-fiction and picture books. They were intended to strike "a steel rapier into the heart of the mass-market Ladybird from which they will never recover", said Sebastian.

As a rule he did not believe in advertising, but an exception was made for these and about £130,000 was spent – in vain, as the books did not sell. They were probably too up-market in approach and design, and, being higher priced than Ladybird, did not, in fact, compete. Sebastian put it down to bad marketing; whatever the reason, heads had to roll. The first of what might be called "the prima donna sackings" took place at Walker Books – of the sales manager.

It has often been wondered why Sebastian could not just sack people, as they have to be sacked in the life of any company, without a drama. One of his faults was complaining about people behind their backs and it is likely that by the time he had decided to sack them he had built up a head of rage which overflowed uncontrollably. There was something almost operatic about the way he set about it, at speed, almost before they had time to catch their breath, not listening to their point of view, and always with shouting and fury. Beware the wrath of the wizard when his spells go wrong.

The Bed-sitting-room

In 1982 Sebastian turned his back on what he called "the bric-a-brac mentality" and moved from his house in North London to a bed-sitter in Holland Park – at least that is how he liked to describe it, defining a bed-sitter as somewhere you can hear the refrigerator humming while lying in bed. His was in fact a studio house on two-and-a-half floors, the half being a bathroom and bedroom in the gallery above the large studio.

Sebastian moved there because "I wanted to be very efficient about domesticity. I had this big family house and I couldn't bear all those closed doors on children who didn't exist, so I thought the best thing for a bachelor was to live in one big room!"

It was a dramatic room, situated on the first floor of one of several houses built as studios by devotees of the extraordinarily popular nineteenth-century artist Lord Leighton, whose own exotic creation, Leighton House, is two doors away. Sebastian bought the house by using his habitual tactics of stunning the vendor into selling by offering him more money than he had dreamt of. It was decorated in a floridly fashionable style complete with marble fireplace and "frilly knicker" blinds. Sebastian's style was the opposite, an imaginatively stream-lined simplicity to play up the space rather than to reduce it with clutter.

His example was the New York "loft" belonging to his friend Joanna Steichen, widow of Edward Steichen, the pioneering photographer. He told his architects, Peter Inskip and Peter Jenkins, with whom he had shared Hanway House, that he wanted a shower, but not a study, and plenty of room to entertain. Beyond that, says Peter Inskip, he had no clear stylistic idea of what he wanted the space to look like.

Sebastian's "bed-sitting-room" in Holland Park, individual and stylish, but not cosy

"From sharing an office with him I had seen his respect for authors and illustrators and that is how he behaved towards us. He put himself totally in our hands. He got wonderful results from his authors and illustrators by trusting them to do their best and that is what I like to think he got from us."

With allusions to the Maison de Verre in Paris and its variable spaces, they designed the ultimate bed-sitting-room. The gallery undulated round two walls, and within it were a bedroom, looking out over the gardens next door, a large free-standing, claw-footed bath with an outsize shower which could be glimpsed from below. Sebastian went with the architects to Paris for the day to choose furniture designed by Eileen Gray, then, as now, a rarified taste, which was being reproduced in small quantities. They chose a capacious sofa, which many visitors found to be the only comfortable place to sit; also a grey, black and white abstract patterned rug, and two Transat chairs, of leather and black lacquered wood, so called because their shape was based on the Cunard line deck chairs. Lowering oneself into a curved Transat chair while holding a flute of champagne, not to mention a conversation, was a preliminary obstacle to be overcome chez Sebastian, as was leaning your head back on the assumption that there was something on which to support it; there wasn't.

In the centre of the room was the magnificent 1930s Steinway concert grand piano which Sebastian bought for himself when Walker Books began to take off, while the Bechstein baby grand went downstairs to the ground floor which contained another bedroom and a room intended one day to be a gallery for the pictures Sebastian had started to collect. Upstairs there was hardly a book to be seen, but downstairs there were two large floor-to-ceiling bookcases with the now-spurned cookery books, his English text books from school, his French texts from Oxford, and books by friends, none of which he ever threw away, whether or not he read them.

Such colour and pattern as there were came from the pictures, and the flowers which were arranged by Julia Hodgkin, at that time married to the artist Howard Hodgkin; they were both friends of Sebastian. She was establishing herself as an original and imaginative florist. The arrangements she did in the understated vases were restrained and elegant rather than outsize, extravagant bunches. In this house even the flowers knew their place.

At the far end of the room was a long, scrubbed oak, eighteenth-century dining-table which came from the Hall at King's College, Cambridge, with a pair of benches. From curving one's spine into an S-shape for the Eileen Gray chairs it had to be held rigidly upright for the benches. A frequent guest, Clementine Beit, wrote to Sebastian, "I like the monastic idea, but the spine tires on the benches if one sits for a long time", and eventually simple black chairs were introduced.

There was no clutter − and no cooking. From being happy to spend hours at a time in the kitchen before having people to dinner, Sebastian had now turned his back on the stove. The fridge held only champagne. "Being efficient about domesticity" meant no shopping, either. No more elaborate creations with dollops of thick cream, no more standing by the caramel thermometer or drizzling melted chocolate onto rich puddings. No more stuffing or basting, whipping or tasting. He entertained as much as ever, but his cook stocked his freezer full of meals and all he had to do was to serve them.

"That sparseness of his surroundings fell down when one reached the table," remembered Nicola Bayley, "which was always beautifully laid, with candles, very elegant, but not blowsy, flowers, capacious white damask napkins, exquisite, plain seventeenth- and eighteenth-century silver to complement the plain white porcelain plates and simple, very fine glasses."

Sebastian lived in his bed-sitter alone; some while before moving he had parted from Donald, each accusing the other of infidelity to such an extent that infidelity seemed hardly the issue. Their friend and confidante Joanna Steichen remembers that "Donald felt shut out; Sebastian didn't confide in him" when Walker Books was starting. "Sebastian was a genius, but he had no conception of other people's feelings. He had no idea of the kind of communication one might need in a relationship so that I can understand that Donald must have felt that he was pretty cold.

"Sebastian understood enough about people to know how to get the best work out of them, one might even say the best yield, that to pamper staff is so important, but he didn't really understand much of anything else about them.

"An emotional education is entirely different from an intellectual education. His inability to tune in to other people's emotions was not necessarily a homosexual characteristic, it was more individual. In fact, it was more like a heterosexual man. In his personal life Sebastian wanted people to be like dolls on a shelf that you took down when you needed them and then put them back when you didn't"; the corollary of which is that if a doll wanted to stay where it was it was not popular.

Joanna Steichen, Sebastian's New York confidante, widow of the photographer Edward Steichen

Although affectionate and generous, Sebastian still found intimate relationships difficult. It was almost as if part of him did not want them, fearful of the demands they would make on him, or that the demands he made of them would not be met. It was not just that he was unwilling to fulfil these demands, he wasn't, necessarily, but he seemed almost afraid of being incapable of doing so, or that these demands would show up some inadequacy or some vulnerability within him.

Sebastian always remained bitter about the ending of his relationship with Donald; it was, after all, the longest-lasting liaison of his life. But now, in his thirty-eighth year, something altogether more exciting happened to him: he fell in love with a woman.

Strictly speaking, she fell in love with him. It is not hard to see why: attractive, intelligent, generous, rich and fond of women, he was a marvellous companion; and of course his never having been intimately attached to a woman played no small part in his attraction for her. She was married, childless and attractive and she made great play for him. They had an intense affair but it could not lead to anything permanent, and eventually it came to an end.

To Sebastian it was a turning-point: he began to wonder if one day he would get married and have the children he longed for. Being the kind of person he was, he wondered this aloud and at length, canvassing his friends and even his acquaintances as to the chances and the desirability of his settling down with a woman. At Matthew and Maro Spender's house in Tuscany after the Bologna Book Fair in 1982 the question was debated morning, noon and night by the entire household, lying out in the spring sunshine, at mealtimes, under the stars; even the white doves seemed to be cooing their opinions.

The question was never to be answered. He had another serious relationship with a woman, over a decade older than himself. He embraced heterosexuality with all the enthusiasm he had previously brought to homosexuality; it was fun, and he enjoyed it. As ever impatient, he was cautioned by the sagacious Clementine Beit that "...the most important thing for you at the moment is not to be in a hurry. What has happened is a momentous change, and it is a time to take stock and have a breather! Don't look on every young woman you meet as either a potential girlfriend or wife."

Although Sebastian lived alone in his bed-sit he was rarely on his own. He entertained constantly – publishers from abroad, authors and illustrators, as well as friends. On one's arrival, the modest front door in the mews would be opened by a remote control buzzer upstairs; at the top of the narrow grey-carpeted stairs Sebastian would be outlined against the window, a slender figure, invariably wearing a white shirt from Turnbull and Asser open at the neck, and a pair of tailored trousers (gone were the frivolous flounces and brocades of previous years). He would proffer a delicate flute of champagne.

It was always the same champagne, Sainsbury's vintage, for it was now – in the mid-80s, halfway through the Thatcher decade – that Sebastian engineered the biggest coup of his career as a children's book publisher: selling books in Sainsbury's supermarkets.

Helen Oxenbury's sharp eye observed Sebastian's ever-increasing success.

Marketing Literacy

At the beginning of his career as an independent publisher Sebastian memorably remarked, "One felt the whole market was a bit of a gap, really." This is what exhilarated him and this is where his genius lay, in spotting which gaps were markets. Now he made the imaginative leap of deciding that the something small and desirable sold to children, or rather to their parents, as they left supermarkets should be books rather than sweeties. Having spent the last seven years producing books of the highest possible standard and selling them all over the world, it seemed a logical step for Sebastian to overcome popular resistance to entering bookshops by bringing books to a place everyone finds themselves regularly – the supermarket.

Sebastian admired Sainsbury's for their insistence on top quality at reasonable prices; and he admired too their high profile in the retailing market, representing dependability and good value. They were to food retailing what Walker Books was to children's book publishing, as one journalist pointed out.

"In its combination of quality and mass marketing Walker Books invites comparison less with other publishing houses than with companies in different fields altogether – with the early days of Disney, say, or of High Street moguls like Conran and

Sainsbury," wrote the magazine *Books for Keeps* in January 1985, words which must have been music to Sebastian's ears (and which in fact he probably uttered in the first place).

Susie Sainsbury, cousin by marriage of the then chairman, had known Sebastian since they worked together fifteen years previously at Jonathan Cape. She recalls Sebastian discussing his idea with her, not over lunch but, typically, at the exercise class they both attended in Notting Hill Gate. While they were vigorously doing their exercises Sebastian asked Susie about his approach to Sainsbury's: should he talk to Sir John Sainsbury, the chairman, direct?

"I said he should definitely approach it from the top – John's an enormous enthusiast – and not just float the idea, but work out the titles, a detailed package.

"Sebastian saw that Sainsbury shoppers were the type of people who bought books. Their own-label cookery books had sold well and this gave Sainsbury the confidence to try these."

Walker Books prepared a very detailed scheme, bearing in mind that it was not for a bookshop, but a supermarket. Their audience was the very young pre-reader, and the books, jolly, colourful, spacious, had all the Walker trademarks. They were the work of such top artists as Helen Oxenbury, John Burningham and Nicola Bayley.

Sainsbury's launched the books, costing from 75p to only £1.25, and they adapted their well-known slogan to "Good Books Cost Less at Sainsbury's" and "Now Sainsbury's Feed the Mind". In deference to the tender age of their customers the books were billed as non-toxic (begging the question of what a toxic book is like). Walker books for health!

Sebastian was delighted as the books sold and sold in their millions. It seemed to confirm his position as a purveyor of popular culture, more than just a profitable publisher, someone who encouraged the progress of literacy. *The Financial Times* reported: "he believes ... 'There's an ethical thing to selling children's books. We're marketing literacy.'"

Sections of the book trade, however, thought they were simply undercutting bookshops, which made the short-lived slogan *Good Books Cost Less at Sainsbury's* particularly unfortunate. A leading bookshop chain, Blackwells, banned Walker books, and others followed suit. Sebastian claimed that selling in a supermarket was actually an encouragement to book-buying generally: "I still feel strongly that the more books that are sold, the more will be required."

After a year Blackwell's started stocking a small number of Walker books – out of consideration to customers and authors, they said, rather than to the publisher. One of their shop managers said in an interview with *The Guardian* that "It was quite a traumatic time. It can be difficult selling children's books and having a big children's department is quite often an act of faith. It may sound a bit odd but we felt betrayed."

The article itself broadly agreed with Sebastian, that in the long run booksellers would be pleased to have the extra book-buying public; and certainly such subsequent successes as Waterstone's chain of bookshops, which are open on Sunday and late into the evenings, would support flexible retailing practices, especially in a recession.

It was in America, where he sold a great many books, that Sebastian had learnt so much about what the market would bear. He liked selling books to Americans, they understood selling, and that selling anything involved selling oneself, too. He admired American professionalism as much as he considered the amateurishness of the British to be their besetting sin. Sebastian spent a lot of time in America; he liked New York, where the fast pace suited someone as easily bored as he was.

Whether they liked him or not, all the American publishers he had dealings with agreed on one thing – Sebastian was unlike any other English publisher. "He changed the manner in which books were sold abroad," says Janet Schulman, vice president of Books for Young Readers at Random House and Alfred Knopf. "Walker Books really did a proper, detailed presentation, as finished as possible, sometimes with proofs, sometimes with original artwork. They always took you through it, and had definite schedules, royalty-inclusive (i.e. there were no further sums to be done) so you could work out the figures immediately and you knew what it would cost you. This, too, was shrewd because it meant that instead of having to go away and work things out and ending the meeting with 'We'll get back to you', buyers were able and inclined to make up their minds on the spot and so Sebby would have a deal. If you have a cooling-off period that is when you can re-evaluate and say, 'I can live without this book.'

"He insisted on selling publishers finished copies of books, not pages to make into books themselves, or just the film, as other publishers did, and so he could mark the book up, rather than the buyers marking the book up themselves in its progress towards being finished.

"He was the opposite of Tom Maschler in terms of approach. Tom was very loud and manic and waved his arms about. Sebastian would be very quiet and quick and just stare at you after he had made his presentation; but somehow you would feel 'I don't want to miss out on this illustrator.'

"In this way and in others he differed from the rest of English publishers: they were totally disorganized. They might give you a jacket proof of the book they were trying to sell you with nothing inside, a typewritten manuscript, maybe a bit of artwork, but no figures worked out: so you couldn't conclude a deal there and then. Sebastian had all of this done.

"Walker Books revolutionized the British system of creating and marketing books: it put the emphasis on marketing as much as on creating."

Sebastian's relationships with many of his American publishers became, characteristically, personal friendships: Janet Schulman, who has been in children's publishing for over thirty years, relates that she first met him in 1982 on her way to Bologna. He had been trying and trying to get her boss at Random House, Gerry Harrison, to buy some books, but he had resisted, feeling that they were not right for them. Janet Schulman made time to see Sebastian and he was always grateful for this. They became friends, he regularly invited her to dinner and, while one might say that this was good business, as she points out the people he didn't like he didn't take to dinner.

Going to America twice a year meant that Sebastian had the time and energy to cultivate contacts there. Another publisher whose judgement he deferred to was Margaret McElderry. Now in her eighties, she has been in the business since 1945. A slender, upright woman, with a low, cultivated voice, she said that for her Sebastian "carried on the tradition of publishers like Jonathan Cape, who was distinguished and idiosyncratic and his method of doing business was very personal.

Janet Schulman,
then editor-in-chief of
Books for Children,
Random House,
New York

"Now publishing has become the business of corporate men who don't really know about books, only products. If a book makes money they are pleased, if it doesn't they can't imagine why it is published."

From the beginning of his publishing career, Sebastian called on this doyenne of New York publishing; he always showed everything to her, and she was flattered by that. She had a comparatively small list, her own imprint within Macmillan New York, so she bought very little, but still Sebastian wanted to show his list to the woman who had introduced such English classics as *The Borrowers* and *Mary Poppins* into America.

Apart from anything else, Margaret McElderry felt that market conditions in America were right for his baby and children's books. The baby boom and increased affluence meant that "Yuppy" parents, educated and professional, wanted their children to be super-geniuses – and the first step towards that was buying books.

A fillip to the selling of children's books was the expansion, coast-to-coast, of children's-book-only bookshops. There are now several hundred such stores, started by dedicated people, ex-teachers and librarians.

As John Keller, of Little, Brown publishers in Boston said, "There was an enormous euphoria in the children's book market. Retail was starting to burgeon, one was more prepared to take a bit of a flier to Sebastian... At Bologna most of the Walker books looked like pearls among a lot of ash."

This had its downside: overselling. This is a puzzling phenomenon to outsiders who reflect that a publisher does not *have* to buy an excessive quantity of a title so that they are stuck with stock they cannot

Margaret McElderry, the publisher, at home in Rhode Island. Sebastian always showed her his new titles.

shift; he is not compelled to buy any at all. John Keller explained: "The stuff looked so good that you, as the buyer, thought you were just as clever as paint to buy it. He would say, 'There is other interest.' Then you'd say, 'Would twenty thousand do it?'

"It was the personality as well as the product, the Oxford accent that came rolling across the desk at you from this clever, slightly eccentric man who was very charming if he wished to be.

"We have a lot of books that came from Walker in our warehouse. All of us could have said 'No'…"

Sebastian always wanted an American office for Walker Books. He offered Janet Schulman and Gerry Harrison the job of setting it up. Was that naiveté, to imagine that they would want to leave their high-powered jobs at Random House, or was it shrewdness to let them know that if they were in the least bit discontented they could join him? "We didn't take the offer terribly seriously, but we didn't laugh at it either," was Janet's comment.

Amy Ehrlich, editor-in-chief of Candlewick Press, Walker Books' sister company

Eventually, in 1990, the American branch of Walker Books, Candlewick Press, was started in Cambridge, Massachusetts, with David Ford in charge. Amy Ehrlich, an experienced editor and writer, was editor-in-chief. When David Ford left to set up his own, brilliantly successful, bookshop-café in his native Georgia, Rick Richter, of sales and marketing, became president.

Fantasy Becomes Reality

Sebastian was a fantasist, but though his head might be in the clouds his feet were on the ground. He had fantasized about being the biggest and best children's book publisher in the world. Now he was, thanks to unceasing work on his part and on the part of the talented team he inspired. He had moved the ever-expanding Walker Books into practical, if idiosyncratic, premises; he himself lived in a very individual style in the ultimate bed-sitting-room designed to suit a rich bachelor with no domestic responsibility. Sebastian loved titles and he had an abundance of them, both among his friends and on Walker Books' list.

Yet it seemed as if he had spent years concentrating on building something up, on giving it a strong identity, only to lose sight of his own. He had expected Walker Books to give him immense satisfaction, and it did, but it also left him insecure, wondering who he was and where he was going. It was also, of course, totally demanding. Despite his loyal team, he alone had responsibility for the company; the risks were his, mistakes were his, decisions were his. He had constructed some imagined opponent to whom he had to prove that he could be successful. He had proved it over and over again, but he was not content. It is trite to say of successful men that their success does not bring them happiness: in

Sebastian's case this was true, but then what would have brought him happiness? His was not a particularly happy temperament.

"He certainly had very large ambitions; it used to fascinate me what would ever satisfy him, at what point would it be apparent that he had reached whatever it was that he was trying to reach? But my theory is that that was just not possible. He was trying to fill some gap within himself that was for ever unsatisfied," says David Ford, who was by now Managing Director.

"I remember saying to him, 'Sebastian, what is it that you want? What is there that's ever going to make you happy?'

"And he said, 'I want to be Walt Disney!'

"I was fascinated by what would come of it all, at what point would he reach satisfaction..." He reiterates what Sebastian often declared, that he had no financial ambition for himself; his ambition was for his family, his nephews and nieces. So, money was not the end; publishing had yielded him success, but Sebastian was neither happy nor satisfied.

Part of the problem was that Walker Books had become, as it had to be, his life; apart from the piano he had no diversions. Having cut domesticity to a minimum, he never cooked, as he used to. He was cooked for, otherwise he ate out.

He always had a favourite restaurant; currently it was the Brasserie St Quentin, opposite the Brompton Oratory, in Knightsbridge. Didier, the maître d', was as attractive as the menu and Sebastian used to chat away in French about the plats du jour. He never, as a matter of principle, it seemed, ate the set menu, but always à la carte; even if he *wanted* to eat only the set menu he would resolutely choose something else as well. For an aperitif he always had a Kir Royale (champagne with cassis) and often ordered the wine in advance so that it could be opened for his arrival.

As for any recreation, such as holidays, he was not really interested in them. He could not see much point in the English countryside: the climate was unpredictable, going for a walk was a penance, unless to a nice food shop or a restaurant. The seaside was equally distasteful, except in a warm climate with sandy beaches and lots of attractive bodies on them. He did like country houses and getting to know their occupants, the grander the better. Sightseeing tended to be done at the double before retiring to a pub or restaurant.

One summer in Norfolk, he could not be got out of the car to visit a stately home, he was so busy listening to Kenneth Williams reading the *William* stories by Richmal Crompton on tape which had been put on for the children; *they* all obediently got out and went round the house as instructed while Uncle Sebby sat in the car giggling, to the bemusement of holiday-makers.

Outside Walker Books, music was the one thing which absorbed him; his staff were used to his spending hours playing the piano. Sometimes they were afraid that it would take up all his time. In the event it was not music which carried him off but, in the summer of 1986, a prolonged nervous breakdown. When, thin and hollow-eyed, he left the nursing-home, he went to join his family on the coast of Norfolk for the summer holidays. He hired a grand piano, went for occasional walks to buy sweeties at the delicatessen in the village, or to the walled vegetable

Norfolk, summer idyll, 1986. Sebastian preparing samphire with his niece, Stella, aged two

garden where he spent sunlit hours grazing, like Peter Rabbit, on tender new carrots, parsley and, later on, mulberries – and there was no Mr McGregor to chase him out of that secret paradise. Every evening before dinner one bottle at least of his favourite Sainsbury's vintage champagne was opened.

The beach was avoided and as for swimming, God forbid! He discovered The Moorings, a wonderful restaurant at Wells-next-the-Sea, where he treated his young nephews and nieces, his party trick being to hand them each five pounds in between courses so they could run across the road to the rock shop and buy false teeth and eggs and bacon made of rock.

Sebastian's Norfolk haven, The Moorings restaurant, Wells-next-the-Sea, painted by Brian Lewis, and (right) with his youngest nephew, David

Every morning he played the piano in the drawing-room, the music floating out over the sunken garden, where the bees sucked on rosemary and lavender and tall yews cast long shadows. It was an idyllic place to get better, but his recovery took a long time.

He kept up with work by telephone. The expanding company needed new premises. He was negotiating for a mattress factory south of the river, in Vauxhall. It was large, forty-two thousand square feet being more than Walker Books needed, and Sebastian's most ambitious purchase to date, costing £2,000,000 for the freehold. He had the foresight to see how the unwieldy industrial premises could be transformed into smart offices for Walker Books.

Proudly he showed people round the new building, stepping across the unpromising spaces with the well-known gleam in his eye. He even fantasized about living above the shop himself, on the top floor with a roof garden. He liked to describe it as "opposite the Tate Gallery" but it is in fact a pretty bleak area, full of outsize office blocks and unprepossessing blocks of flats.

The mattress factory soon had its own identity as the headquarters of Walker Books. The formula was the same as before, white walls with bright colours elsewhere. The dining-room for the staff was larger than ever, with various small rooms off it for working lunches. The number of staff was to rise to around a hundred. As there were few shops or other amenities in the area they were pleased to be able to have lunch on the premises; some of them even felt that Sebastian had deliberately chosen an area with few distractions to take them away from work.

Sebastian ate there every day. He was never "out to lunch". When he was invited he would say, "I'm not very good at going out to lunch," and instead ask people for "a spot of lunch" at Vauxhall Walk. His office was a large room on the ground floor, its singularly bare desk testifying to his preference for doing business over the telephone. One wall was covered with much-prized pictures given him by illustrators.

The mattress factory, Vauxhall, South London, as it is now and as it was. The Walker Bear (inset), designed by Helen Oxenbury

The factory was an aggressively no-smoking zone. Sebastian issued an unequivocal memo to that effect:

> As you will see from the sign that Alan has put up on our door this morning, Walker Books has become a NO SMOKING building.
>
> As the company has got bigger so has my distress at watching those of my beloved colleagues who smoke inflict this serious health risk upon themselves. It is the realization that you will only stop when one of you has a fatal illness that makes me, for the first time in our ten-year history, issue you all with an order.
>
> Most of you really long to give up which is why there is no "smoking room" in the building. If any of you are overwhelmed with the urge to smoke I am quite happy for you to do so in the street (preferably in the gutter where such activity belongs). When it is raining you will be allowed to smoke under the arch, provided you stub the cigarette out in the street – it would be unfair to ask Ted and Barbara to have to clean up your fag ends every day from our property.
>
> There are no ashtrays except two held by Jos. Visitors may smoke if they ask to do so, and must ask her for an ashtray and return it to her when they have finished. I have appointed two vigilantes to each floor whom I have empowered to remove a cigarette that they find lit anywhere. They are, on my floor – Jenny and Patsy, on the second floor – Steve and Julia, on the first floor Jos and on the ground floor Alan and Bill. All vigilantes will have a supply of nicotine chewing gum.
> Love and good luck,
>   SEB

Pseud's Corner, in *Private Eye*, gleefully reproduced this.

Another children's book imprint had come to join Walker Books. This was Julia MacRae Books, highly respected, with a distinguished list, mainly of fiction by such distinguished authors as Rumer Godden, Janni Howker and Jane Gardam, and some illustrated books, notably by Anthony Browne. She wrote to Sebastian, "I am utterly bowled over by your

company. The sense of commitment, professionalism, enthusiasm, and enjoyment here is overwhelming, and within a few hours of arriving I knew for certain that I was going to be very happy indeed. The style of this company bears eloquent witness to a real genius for management, and I am deeply impressed by the universal loyalty and affection there so clearly is for you and David. I have been extraordinarily fortunate to land here, and will do my utmost to make it a worthwhile investment from your point of view."

Sebastian also took on another individual imprint – Nick Hern Books, which published not children's books, but theatrical texts. Sebastian could rarely resist an enterprising individual with a good idea and in this case his hope was that there would eventually be a crossover between the theatrical texts for grown-ups and some for children, but in the event this did not happen.

A rooftop room in the factory was given to one of Walker Books' favourite author-artists, Colin McNaughton, producer of such books as *There's an Awful Lot of Weirdos in Our Neighbourhood*.

Walker Books' identity was further established on

Colin McNaughton, dressing the part on a promotional tour for Captain Abdul's Pirate School (top, right) and reading at a primary school (centre)

Hee-haw-hee-haw-hee-haw

the publishing scene when Helen Oxenbury designed a colophon of a bear holding a candle. The bear appeared in many other guises, among them as a wooden Christmas card and painted on a large sign hanging outside the erstwhile mattress factory. Sebastian loved the Walker bear: innocent and wise, childish and patriarchal, it put the ultimate seal of identity on his enterprise. He would doubtless have had it embroidered on his linen at home if he could; was he joking when he told his nephews and nieces that Uncle Sebby's bear could be incorporated into their family coat of arms? More to the point, the bear, at once timeless and up-to-date, its candle illuminating the surrounding darkness, made

Sebastian and his driver, Noel, and the Walker Bear taxi

his company immediately recognizable. Its most original appearance was on the side of the Walker Books' taxi, a black London cab driven by Sebastian's devoted chauffeur, Noel. (Sebastian had realized it was time he gave up driving after he had steered his car straight into a wall after a very merry wedding in the country.)

Sebastian now had on his list every children's book author he wanted except three: Roald Dahl, Janet Ahlberg and Maurice Sendak. Dahl he never acquired, despite persuasive overtures; Sendak did work for Walker Books. Like many of Sebastian's professional relationships this one too became intensely personal; based on admiration – Sebastian yielded to none in his admiration for Sendak – it soon became shot through with affection.

Sebastian called *Where the Wild Things Are* "the greatest children's book of the century"; of *Dear Mili*, a Grimm's fairy tale illustrated by Sendak, he said, "the pictures glow with mystery and rapture … the lyrical and romantic side of Sendak's art." He also admired his perfectionism: "Tantalizingly Sendak remains very private and we learn nothing of the technical demands he has placed upon himself. When Richter makes a mistake (Statislav Richter, the pianist) he repeats the passage at the keyboard two hundred times: I wonder what Sendak does."

Like Sendak, Sebastian was aware of the connection between music and illustration: "It takes time to tell a story in pictures, just as it does to play a piece of music. As both are interpretative arts, both must unfold, often with their own tempi markings. The pulse of a visual narrative is comparable to rhythm in music," he wrote in *The Telegraph* in May 1989.

Sebastian pinpointed what is most characteristic of Sendak's work, what gives it its excitement and tension, "the unsettled harness between the secret and poetic on the one hand, and the earthy impertinence on the other". That is what Sebastian responded to in the best children's literature, the secrecy and poetry of childhood recaptured by an artist and coupled with the exuberant, vulgar cheek only permissible in childhood.

To be described in such terms can only have disposed Sendak favourably towards Sebastian. The two had more in common than might at first be thought of between a Brooklyn-raised son of Polish emigrants, who left school as soon as he was able, and an Oxford-educated publisher-businessman. For a start, both men chose to live on their own, Sebastian in his pared-down studio house, Sendak in the woods of Connecticut, where his house, with "its deliberate cheery coziness … its Audubon prints and whirligigs, its wood floors and toy soldiers, is another of his inventions," as one journalist described it.

Both men were at the top of their professions, and well aware of it; both were complicated, emotional, private men and yet in many ways transparently simple. Both of them were emotional, yet almost dispassionately rational; private, and at the same time gregarious. Magnetic, atttracting both men and women, while also keeping them at a distance. In both their lives music was central. They first met at Glyndebourne, at a rehearsal of *Where the Wild*  *Things Are*, Sendak's celebrated book transformed into an opera with sets designed by himself. Sebastian wasted no time in working on him, using all the blandishments in his repertoire, a consummate performance which Sendak, as a professional, recognized and, as a human being, responded to.

"He was such a seducer," he recalls. "It was a natural element to him, to swim like a fish in water, to get what he wanted, to do his little Sebastian Walker dance. I'm an old pro, I've been danced to before, but never by such a unique talent. I enjoyed it! I think he knew that I knew, because he knew I was a canny old guy. I'd heard such awful things about him; when I went back home and said that I was going to do a book

Maurice Sendak (left) and below, Tail Feathers From Mother Goose, *for which he designed the cover, 1988.*
Iona Opie (above), the noted collector and editor of children's rhymes

for Sebastian Walker people immediately said, 'Don't trust him. He's a cheat ... a liar ... a crook.' My lawyer said, 'He's the last man to be trusted ... he rolls you over, he's a conniver.' They all thought I had been literally seduced by his charm and you know it was sheer hard jealousy: he'd come to America with a flash smile and he'd leave the country waving his cheque book."

The opportunity arose for Sendak to do some work for Sebastian when an appeal for the Opie collection was launched. This outstanding collection of children's books and related material, dating back to medieval times and going up to the present day, was formed over forty years by Peter and Iona Opie. A few years after Peter Opie's death in 1982, his widow launched an appeal for £500,000, which she herself matched, to secure the collection for the Bodleian Library in Oxford. This was exactly the sort of project that appealed to Sebastian, involving as it did children's books, Oxford and the chance for Walker Books to be seen to be doing good. He responded immediately, swooping down to Oxford for lunch in his bear-adorned taxi in March 1987. All eyes, thin and drawn, he seemed to the appeal organizers more like a creature from another planet than the foremost children's book publisher of the day.

His hostess, Gillian Avery, is a noted cook. "Yum!" said Sebastian, tucking in to the *tomates en gêlée* and the *vitello tonnato* which followed, talking very little, except about his piano when he chatted on about what pieces he was playing. Only towards the third course, an iced hazelnut parfait, was the subject of the Appeal raised and then he was fizzing with ideas, starting with taking Burlington House and giving everyone delicious things to eat and drink and continuing with the Albert Hall.

Eventually the best, and most productive, idea was hit upon, a book, *Tail Feathers From Mother Goose*, which was published in 1988. It consisted of rhymes from the Opie archive, mostly unpublished, each one illustrated by a leading artist and designed into an elegant whole by Amelia Edwards. The cover was by Maurice Sendak. It showed Mother Goose resplendent in striped gown and feathered hat.

After *Tail Feathers* was published Sebastian flew by Concorde to New York, taking Iona Opie with him for the American publication. He stayed with Joanna Steichen and then with Sendak. As chronically insecure people do, he mapped out, in his imagination, a permanent part for himself in Sendak's life. He fantasized about living with him there in the house in the woods; he would play the piano which Sendak had recently inherited, bring Noel over to drive him round: "It was a total little fantasy," said Sendak. He himself was realistic about this side of Sebastian because, he said, "His whole life was a fantasy, but the word you're missing here is that he was an artist. That's the central thing. As an artist he was a great juggler. He juggled reality and fantasy with incredible ability, standing on a high wire over a canyon, and he said: 'I can do this because I've such an ego, it's bigger than the whole canyon.' He had to see if it could all work and not destroy him. That is the artist. I think he was an extraordinarily creative man. This is what intrigued me so much. He had a formidable array of acts, I mean really genuine creative

...ts, everything he did had such a finish, a polish and beauty to it, and what radiated out of it was his extraordinary kindness." None of which blinded Sendak to his shortcomings, in particular his magnificent snobbery which seemed to increase with every year that passed.

"It was so ostentatious it was like a creative interest. He was totally unashamed about it, you couldn't shame him, I tried my best to do so. That was the charm, he wasn't going to let anybody paint him into a corner about life."

Sendak also recognized the central solitariness of Sebastian's life, a *sine qua non* of his existence; and the paradox of an insecure, vulnerable man, whose need for love was insatiable, but who nevertheless "put the shutters up" at once if he felt himself about to be swamped, as he saw it, by another's affection.

The somewhat unexpected trio of Sendak, Sebastian and Iona Opie were to come together again before long; but after *Tail Feathers From Mother Goose*, says Sendak, "Though he wanted me to do a book, for a long time there wasn't anything purposeful for me to do. Unless we could do something unique and grand there was no point in us doing it, and he approved of that, but at the same time because of his business savvy it drove him crazy!"

"Tell It Again and Tell It the Same"

The astonishing range of talented artists who contributed to *Tail Feathers From Mother Goose*, from those like Helen Oxenbury, Nicola Bayley and Colin McNaughton, who had been with Walker Books since the early days, to the many later recruits – Jill Murphy, Angela Barrett, Fritz Wegner and Charlotte Voake, Patrick Benson, Michael Foreman and Helen Craig, to mention only a few – showed how far Walker Books had come since it was just a gleam in Sebastian's eye ten years before. Among them, one was to make a significant difference to its fortunes. Martin Handford was the creator of Wally, an amiable character in bobble hat and round glasses who soon had an immense following across the world in such books as *Where's Wally?* and *Where's Wally Now?*

Like the board books before them, the Wally books' huge success resulted from a simple idea brilliantly executed: they were as much games as books, appealing to all ages, not just to children; funny and inventive, the crowded pages are crammed with jokey detail. The snappy text moves you briskly from page to page in a way that is helpful to slow readers.

The unassuming Martin Handford was a freelance artist, working for, among other clients, London Transport, and specializing in crowd scenes when Walker Books' art editor David Bennett contacted him. They began work on a book about busy places, then a central character was needed to link the action-packed pages which were Handford's forte. In the words of *The Bookseller*, "Wally was born". After his debut in 1987, Wally was an immediate success and appeared under a variety of aliases – *Waldo* in the USA, *Charlie* in France – in over twenty countries.

Since the first book, *Where's Wally?*, the pictures became more intricate and Wally harder to find. He was joined by his girl-friend, Wenda, and his dog, Woof. But Wally never succumbed to the pretentiousness success often brings. *Where's Wally? The Ultimate Fun Book*, which came out in 1990, had peel-off stickers, press-out figures, all sorts of things Martin Handford said he loved as a child: "That's a prime reason for doing these books – I'm doing something which I know would really have excited me when I was nine years old." What better reason for doing any children's book?

David Bennett, the art editor who assisted the gestation of Wally (below left) by Martin Handford (right), in 1987

Sebastian himself did not have much to do with the money-spinning Martin Handford, except to relish his huge success. "I am devoted to Wally," he said. "He sells in millions" – and brought in millions of pounds, too, which helped to keep lesser-sellers afloat.

At the same time as they launched Wally upon an appreciative public, Walker Books began bringing out teenage novels, for a much smaller readership. Expansion into the older age-group was partly prompted by the arrival at Walker Books of Sebastian's old friend, Selina Hastings, an editor who knew how to get the best out of writers by praising their work lavishly and perceptively while nudging them gently towards the … perhaps … less successful aspects of their manuscripts. This positive approach, and the generous advances which Walker Books customarily paid, soon resulted in an auspicious list of established and first-time authors.

Virginia Ironside's *Vampire Master* is a Gothic comedy of boarding school; Aisling Foster's *The First Time* dealt, with a light touch, with urban teenagers and sex, while the first title to be published, in April 1987, was *Stray*, by A.N. Wilson, the first children's book written by the distinguished novelist and biographer. In fact *Stray* is a success with cat-lovers of all ages, for the author has "the ability to enter into the mind of a cat as completely as into the mind of man, woman and child," as Selina Hastings said. The identification with the creatures in his novel makes for a moving story: "While I was writing it, I was more caught up in the adventure than I have been with any of my previous stories for grown-ups," said the author. It was a *tour de force* by the author who was to go on to write the biographies of Tolstoy and Jesus.

Teenage fiction from established writers was started in 1987, with covers by such illustrators as Mick Brownfield (top) and Sarah Fox-Davies (bottom)

Hugh Scott's novel
Why Weeps the
Brogan?, *1989*
Whitbread Children's
Novel Award; jacket
illustrated by James
Marsh

But for all the quality of the books, the enthusiasm of the reviewers, and the fact that the time was right for well-written fiction for this age-group, this category of book is notoriously difficult to sell. Several authors were very disappointed with the sales, and wondered whether it was that their books did not sell, or that they were not sold?

The best of the teenage-fiction list was imaginative, varied and excellently written, often better, in fact, than fiction for adults. One of the few unsolicited manuscripts to be published, *Why Weeps the Brogan?,* by Hugh Scott, won the Whitbread Children's Novel Award in 1989. That helped to triple its normal hardback sale.

Sebastian himself did not read the novels he published, any more than he read any other novels; he preferred younger children's books because they had less words and more pictures. He made an exception, however, for Virginia Ironside's *Vampire Master,* which he enjoyed greatly.

"He wasn't basically interested in fiction, but on the other hand he realized that a 'grown-up' (i.e. a well-established) publishing house has a fiction list," says Wendy Boase, who took it over when Selina Hastings left. He was proud of publishing *Stray* and furious, jumping up and down on the pavement, when Andrew Wilson suggested that he should take it elsewhere for paperback publication.

"I was so depressed at how badly the list sold,"

Wendy Boase says, "and he said to me, 'Every ten years there will be one wonderful book and that will pay for all the others.'" Whether or not this is true, his encouragement kept her going.

Not until they had an extensive backlist did Walker Books start publishing paperbacks. That was in 1988, when their list rose to an unprecedented 341 titles, from picture books to teenage novels.

"Sebastian didn't believe in peaceful co-existence. The competition was to be wiped out. So the ten per cent royalty which he paid to paperback authors when he started that list was to make life difficult for Puffin, who couldn't afford to pay it but they would just have to – and they did," commented David Ford.

For Walker Books, as it approached the end of its first decade, it was a time of expansion and profit. Illustrators and authors continued to flock to it. Visitors to the mattress factory found it more than ever a-buzz with ideas and projects, the atmosphere confident and cheerful. This buoyancy was underlined in Sebastian's public pronouncements to the press. Ever a master of manipulation, he told reporters who came to interview him as a publishing phenomenon, which indeed he was, exactly what he wanted them to write about him. He presented himself as an enlightened gentleman-publisher concerned with pushing out the boundaries of literacy; with seeing, as he put it, "tiny minds blooming and blossoming with the written word" and with doing his best for the

William Mayne and Patrick Benson, 1984 Mother Goose Award

talented artists and authors he employed. The more profitable Walker Books, the less his concern about "the bottom line". What, me a basking shark waiting to snap up authors and illustrators? Never, he seemed to be saying. Rather, he declared to one journalist, "I will stop at nothing to get the best authors to do their best work."

There was, as always with Sebastian, truth in this: he was only interested in the highest standards; he did believe in a smallish, personal publishing house rather than a faceless public company where all eyes were glued to "the bottom line"; he was visionary in seeing what could be done with his chosen type of book, such as selling in Sainsbury's. Success had, as it generally does, increased his confidence (or emphasized his arrogance, depending on your point of view), a confidence which he expressed in print: "'You really must realize that you can't have one of these every time we come here.' A young mother was addressing her four-year-old daughter, who was clutching a children's book in Sainsbury's. This book 'habit', developed at Sainsbury's, is nothing less than literacy. The four-year-old in question was reacting to a literary children's book in a way, ten years ago, we all imagined she would react only to the television set, or at best to a comic," Sebastian reflected in *The Daily Telegraph* in July 1989.

"The standard of television for children is still dismal. Yet more dismal is the standard of television tie-in books for children, where characters are two-

Selina Hastings and Juan Wijngaard, 1985 Kate Greenaway Award

dimensional cyphers, coyly begging that their familiarity from the screen should be echoed on children's notepaper, lunch-boxes and toothpaste...

"What is literacy? It is the means by which a child can extend its imagination and reasoning into all intellectual disciplines. If that young mother in Sainsbury's dreams of her daughter being a ballerina, a concert pianist, a film star or a surgeon, all of these careers, fanciful and real, depend on her daughter's early steps in literacy.

"Nobody really knows how a child learns to read. In running my own publishing house for children, I have learnt to tread delicately between the competing views and to try and assimilate the most important common factors, and build books with them..."

His resonant conclusion was the one on which Walker Books' standards were based, that "mass appeal and literary quality are not mutually exclusive".

He always included a reference to Sainsbury's in terms which made them seem as much benefactors to the human race as Andrew Carnegie: "'When the history of children's literature is written,' says Sebastian Walker, without the slightest trace of a twinkle in a not infrequently twinkling eye, 'Sainsbury's will be seen as the biggest factor in the book-buying habits of children,' wrote *The Independent* in June 1988.

The Sebastian Walker who put himself over as

Martin Waddell and Barbara Firth, winners of the Smarties Prize, the Kate Greenaway Award and the Emil/Kurt Maschler awards high-minded publisher and business wizard, articulate, witty, side-swiping the competition, was obviously better copy than the usual tycoon in a suit discussing annual turnover:

"The other day, when one of Britain's publishing magnates cast an envious eye at the prolifically successful children's book publishers, Walker Books, he asked its deceptively nonchalant

chairman and founder, Sebastian Walker, if he could buy the firm," related *The Independent*.

"'I said that if he could teach me the Chopin *nocturne* I was learning, I would give him five per cent of the company. I practise two hours a day on the piano, but I'm having a lot of trouble with this one,' was Sebastian's reply."

"In ten years," the article went on, "he has built up the concern started in his back bedroom into one of the few independent British-owned publishing houses in London. It has a ten million pound turnover, half of it in export, the largest number of new children's titles of any publisher, seventy-five employees and new offices down the road from London's Tate Gallery.

"Mr Walker's business acumen, a subject he seems to find profoundly boring compared to his real passions of children's literature and children's writers, must be considerably more acute than he cares to admit. 'Oh, I know it doesn't sound very macho, but I've no personal financial ambitions, absolutely none. I think the financial side is a bore.

"'Most publishers are far too concerned with their company's profit, and there is an awful lot of vainglorious carry-on in publishing. I find it a yawn a minute. I have dinner with an author three times a week, and look forward to it, but I hate the dreaded publisher's lunch. I just couldn't fit in with the bigger firms.'"

Although he claimed to find the financial side of Walker Books "a bore", he was quick off the mark when it started to go askew. In July 1988, just after *The Independent* interview, deciding that he wanted his "independent, author-led, slightly eccentric company" put "into economic shape" he appointed an old Oxford friend, Kate Mortimer, as chief executive. He, meanwhile, took off to spend more time at the keyboard and stepped back from day-to-day management.

This was the sole occasion on which Sebastian deviated from his personal style of management. It did not work. Miss Mortimer was an experienced and highly regarded monetary theoretician, on the main board of Rothschild's and a member of the Think Tank; she was not experienced in publishing nor in marketing. Her approach was, predictably, entirely different from Sebastian's. The results were disastrous: acrimonious sacking in October 1989; desk cleared; contents sent to Mortimer residence in plastic dustbin sack; pretax profits almost halved – in the year to June 30, 1989, they stood at £243,000 (1988, £433,000).

The experiment was not repeated.

Michael Rosen and Helen Oxenbury won the Smarties Prize in 1989. Helen won it again, with Martin Waddell, in 1991.

"As I leave the Walker warehouse," wrote the journalist Valerie Grove a few months later in the *Sunday Times*, "I reflect that this Utopia of flowers, teddy bears and happy smiling people, and millions of lovely pounds rolling in, has its share of dragons and crocodiles with snapping jaws. There have been shattered nerves (including Walker's) and internecine tensions… The short-lived reign of Kate Mortimer, late of the Rothschild Think Tank, as chief executive, was not a happy time for anyone. Walker refers to her waspishly as 'the pea-brained intellectual'."

Perhaps it would have been more germane to question not her ability to do the job but the wisdom of her appointment to head a firm used to Sebastian's particularly idiosyncratic leadership.

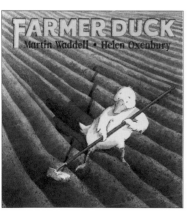

Sebastian declared that he despised prizes. But Walker Books attracted a fair amount, which were encouraging for the firm and for its authors and artists. The first prize-winning books were William Mayne's Hob Books, for which Patrick Benson won the Mother Goose Award in 1984, his first books for children. The following year Juan Wijngaard's glowing illustrations to *Sir Gawain and the Loathly Lady* won the Kate Greenaway. Prizes were won with regularity thereafter: among the titles were *Can't You Sleep, Little Bear?* by Martin Waddell with illustrations by

Barbara Firth (1988); *We're Going on a Bear Hunt* by Michael Rosen and Helen Oxenbury (1989); *The Park in the Dark* by Martin Waddell and Barbara Firth (1989), while in 1991 *Farmer Duck* by Martin Waddell and Helen Oxenbury won two prizes and Colin McNaughton received the Emil/Kurt Maschler Award for *Have You Seen Who's Just Moved in Next Door to Us?*

Sebastian regarded prizes as a distraction from the central business of producing good books. So were advertising and merchandizing. "I think that merchandizing things with characters from children's books is downright corrupting," he said in an interview; for "all that counts is that a child says at the end of the book, 'Tell it again, and tell it the same.' Then its reputation will spread by word of mouth."

With the exception of the Walker Books taxi with its bear on the side, Sebastian never advertised. He regarded it as the same sort of waste as expensive offices: he did not think that either advertising or publishing parties helped books, although Walker Books gave children's parties. He preferred sponsoring events, putting it quite bluntly, "We do a lot of art sponsorship with the aim of achieving brand recognition." It tended to be musical sponsorship – the Ballet Rambert, Glyndebourne Touring Company.

Colin McNaughton, 1991 Emil/Kurt Maschler Award

For Sebastian, Glyndebourne was always a very special place: partly, he was taken by its individuality, expressing, like his publishing house, the vision of one man, George Christie; it was quintessentially English, yet, like Walker Books, international; everything about it, from the famous gardens to the standard of music, was of the best, yet it was never flashy, despite a whiff of corporate entertaining. On occasion, Sebastian's entertaining at Glyndebourne was a type of corporate entertaining, of favoured illustrators or foreign visitors, besides friends and family.

Sebastian's idea of a perfect summer evening was to leave London for Glyndebourne in mid-afternoon by train or to be driven by Noel, with a hamper of goodies and large amounts of champagne and wine; to stroll around the gardens, glass in hand, before settling down in the auditorium; to saunter out in the interval towards one's well-placed picnic spot. (The placing of picnics on the lawns at Glyndebourne was one of the arcane social rituals of the musical upper classes in which Sebastian delighted, involving as it did a swift walk, almost, but not quite, a run, towards your

chosen spot across the immaculate lawns, the imperceptible jostling of your rivals, and sometimes, caddishly, leaving your empties on their rug at the end to avoid carting them home…)

As far as Sebastian was concerned, the English countryside was at its best surveyed from a picnic rug across the ha-ha at Glyndebourne.

Angela Barrett, illustrator of Martin Waddell's The Hidden House, *which won the W.H. Smith Illustration Award, 1991*

The Publisher and the Piano

The more successful Sebastian became in business the more determined he was to master the keyboard. In fact, he was as single-minded about piano-playing as he was about publishing. He explained to the journalist Valerie Grove: "I mean, one is dealing with Helen Oxenbury, etc., the best in their field, all day and one longs for one's own specialized compartment of achievement." This was in 1984, the year he bought his magnificent Steinway concert grand.

Some rich men collect houses or jewels; he loved pianos. He had pianos all over the world. Some he owned, others were his to play on when he wanted. In New York, Wanda Horowitz arranged for him to play in the Steinway rooms beneath Carnegie Hall, where the concert artists practised. When he stayed in France with his doctor and old friend Patrick Woodcock, a piano would be hired. At Badminton House, staying with the Duke and Duchess of Beaufort, he played in the chandelier-hung ballroom; he had had the grand piano reconditioned for them as a house-warming present when they moved into the big house on the death of the old Duke. In Norfolk his hired grand awaited him. The instrument did not have to be anything special: when he stayed in Stockwell, South London, with Nicola Bayley and John

Hilton he was happy to strum away on their old upright.

He never grudged the time he spent going over and over a passage, a phrase, or a single chord. For an impatient man, the piano might seem the last instrument that he would want to play; but, obsessive, tenacious and perfectionist as he was, this was "a hobby carried to a passionate and wonderful extent", as his American publishing friend Margaret McElderry described it. It was also an attempt to create order, to achieve perfection – and to drive himself to the limit. His relationship with his chosen instrument was the only one in his life which gave him unadulterated pleasure; the piano was the one companion of whom he never tired. Endlessly demanding, endlessly satisfying, while it showed up his faults, it gave him also intellectual stimulus and spiritual satisfaction, presenting a challenge to which he was glad to return over and over again. It was also the perfect corollary to his work at Walker Books.

He was now one of the few amateur pupils of Peter Feuchtwanger, "one of Dame Nature's miraculous pedagogues," Sebastian said – but not quite miraculous enough, it transpired. He made two close keyboard friends among Feuchtwanger's other, professional, pupils – Vivien Banfield and a young Dutchman, David Kuyken. Sebastian proposed that

The Duchess of Beaufort, Sebastian and the Countess of Chichester at the opera festival, Savonlinna, Finland

the three of them should attend Feuchtwanger's master class in July 1984. He bought the tickets and away they all flew to Switzerland, Sebastian loyally taking his music scores in a Sainsbury's carrier bag.

As well as the intensive classes, their time at the hotel in Sion was full of fun and jollity; Sebastian drank David and Vivien's mini-bars dry when they stayed up late, but at the same time Vivien, who became very fond of Sebastian, recognized his overweening desire to excel at the piano, and at the same time that he was not, and never could become, a professional; so that this sort of teaching – "being groomed for stardom", as his friend Patrick Woodcock put it – was not for him.

"He played very beautifully and so much from the heart, but he didn't have much natural facility, a lot of what he did was sheer determination. He didn't seem to be naturally coordinated, there would be a tiny little bit of drift.

"He stood beside the piano when I played for him and he made me play a bit over and over again. He had a wonderful ear, he always knew what worked and what didn't, and he always had something intelligent to say. Sebastian had a more professional attitude and a greater love for music than a lot of professionals.

The pianist Vivien Banfield on the steps of St John Smith's Square, where she and Sebastian often went to recitals

"I used to say that the music he most loved, for example the Haydn sonatas, was written in a period of enlightenment, for gifted amateurs who spent a lot of time at the piano. Haydn said that his music was written for amateurs and connoisseurs."

Besides Haydn, Sebastian had a deep affinity for the music of Bach and his contemporary, Scarlatti, as well as Mozart, Chopin and Liszt. His musical ambition was to be able to play the Schubert B flat sonata. Mendelssohn's rippling chords were the unacceptable voice of Romanticism. He played little modern music.

Sebastian declared to Vivien, "I want to be married to the piano." It was when he accepted that the harmony of his relationship with his chosen instrument depended on his settling for a less ambitious programme of music that it was at its happiest. A little while later, he changed to a teacher, Daniel l'Homme, who was more used to gifted young people than to aspiring professionals. Sebastian scaled down his pieces to a more attainable level, for instance, successfully graduating from Chopin's Nocturnes to his very demanding Polonaise in F sharp minor. He performed that at one of the pupils' concerts which Daniel l'Homme held every summer for admiring parents and friends, when Sebastian would take his place among the talented teenagers, who included the son of Alfred Brendel and the children of Sir Colin Davis. To prepare himself, he would rehearse in front of a close friend, Ruth, Lady Fermoy, or Vivien Banfield – neither of whom were allowed to attend the final concert, however, because "they knew too much". At one of these rehearsals Sebastian placed a chair in the middle of the room and ordered Vivien to sit on it "swinging her legs like a bored eight year old".

Otherwise his piano playing was a solitary pleasure. Every day he would practise for an hour or so before going in to Walker Books and again when he returned home. This discipline suited him, the element of repetition in practising helped to clear his mind, enabling him to focus all the better on his work. He rarely played for friends; like most perfectionists he did not think he was up to a high enough standard. It is also possible that he did not wish to reveal as much of himself as playing in front of other people inevitably would.

He regularly went to piano recitals at the Wigmore Hall and the South Bank, often with Vivien Banfield or with another musical friend he made, Ruth, Lady Fermoy. Even if a recital was disappointing he never walked out but always stayed to the end. There was something interesting even in a bad performance. "He was musical in the way he listened, in the intensity of his aural concentration," says Vivien.

Tatayana Nikolaieva.
Her appearance
as a quintessential
babushka was belied
by her artistic delicacy.

"He hated people who played very correctly and without daring. The music had to live and it had to speak to you. It didn't matter if the interpretation was controversial. It had to work on all levels, spiritually, intellectually and imaginatively."

The performers who achieved this, and who had formed his musical taste, were many of the ones whose records he had bought years before, at school and at Oxford: pianists such as Solomon, Dinu Lipatti and Clara Haskil. Latterly he admired Russian pianists Tatayana Nikolaieva, the close friend of Shostakovitch, whose music, for example the 24 Preludes and Fugues (which were written for her) she played at the Wigmore Hall, where Sebastian went to hear her, and also Piotr Anderszewski playing the Diabelli variations.

With some of the pianists he admired he became

friends – Alfred Brendel, for instance, and his wife, Reni, who lived in Hampstead, and the beautiful Japanese Mitsuko Uchida, whom he was taken to hear when she was playing the complete Mozart piano concerti with the English Chamber Orchestra, conducting them herself from the keyboard. Uchida's star quality was matched by a profound musicality. Sebastian got to know her through mutual friends Sir Fred and Lady Warner. He invited Uchida to Glyndebourne and when she offered to pay something towards the tickets said, "No, I'm so rich, let me take you." Instead he preferred to take up her offer of a lesson on the Haydn sonata he was then learning. Later she was to repay his generosity by playing, unforgettably, a Mozart sonata at his funeral.

One of the few people Sebastian would play to was the very musical Ruth, Lady Fermoy, who became a close friend and confidante. Almost eighty when they met, after a concert in London, she was always elegant, with beautifully dressed white hair and a graceful bearing. She was a close friend of the Queen Mother, whose lady-in-waiting she was, and the grandmother of the Princess of Wales. "The reason he liked being with me," she said with characteristic modesty, "was because I was so old and totally undemanding" – she might have added "and unshockable" for Sebastian was his usual completely uninhibited self even with this elderly lady. She was also appreciative of his generosity and his musicality and soon she made him an offer he found irresistible. Having been one of the founders of the King's Lynn Festival in Norfolk, she now wanted to start another musical project: Music in Country Churches would put on concerts of the highest musical standard during the summer, in aid of country churches, for audiences for whom live performances were not readily available. This scheme had all the ingredients Sebastian liked best – impeccable music, surroundings and social connections. Its patron was the Prince of Wales. It would also be a good outlet for Walker Books' sponsorship.

As usual when he was really interested in something he took it up at once and became deeply involved. The first two concerts were held in the summer of 1989 in Salle Church, Norfolk, one of the loveliest churches in England, rising dramatically out of the flat landscape. The Prince of Wales' red helicopter landed in a nearby field, and he was ushered into the front pew. As the performance

Sebastian at a reception with his musical friend Ruth, Lady Fermoy

progressed, the evening light faded through the tall perpendicular windows and in the roof the bats flickered "like little bits of burnt paper".

Being Sebastian, he fantasized about eventually founding a music festival and envisaged a contented old age helping young musicians who performed at it.

His was never the blanket generosity of the magnate scattering largesse. It was more the magnificent treat, which often included the Walker Books staff, such as when he took a coachload of them to Glyndebourne to hear their repertory company. Time and again he picked up the bill in a restaurant. His favourite restaurant was now Bibendum, in the Michelin building in South Kensington. On the day when Julia Hodgkin, his old friend who arranged his flowers at home, opened up her flower van in the forecourt of the Michelin Building (which, incidentally, has made it one of the prettiest sights in London), Sebastian invited her to have dinner with him there, just the thing to calm her nerves. When his niece won a scholarship to her public school he took her out to lunch at The Ritz. His way of giving was imaginative. "You are so generous, darling, to your friends; few people who become millionaires are as generous as you," wrote Freda Berkeley after a visit to

Julia Hodgkin with her flower van in the courtyard of the Michelin Building, the Fulham Road

A Midsummer Night's Dream at Glyndebourne. For birthday presents he would give close friends or relations a giant pot of caviare or a silk shirt from a Bond Street boutique. Whatever he did he did in style, but without ostentation; none more critical than he of anything that shouted of money; yet, in a typical paradox, he enjoyed being rich and would talk about how "seriously rich" he was far, far more than he would have thought acceptable in anybody else. He was one of the first people to take up the phrase "mega-rich" and apply it, shamelessly, to himself. Only a few people could exclaim "Sebby! Really!" to deflect him from his Mr Toad-like showing off. "I banned money and Badminton," says Patrick Woodcock, who was one of these.

Among his many fantasies was buying a second home, perhaps a red-brick house in North Oxford or a disused church in Norfolk. But when it came down to it he was realistic enough to know that he was best off living as he did in Holland Park, by himself, but with his driver, Noel, and his personal assistant, Jenny Moores, a most sympathetic presence, at the end of a telephone.

As the very rich do, he spent money on simplifying his life, on saving time by, for instance, making telephone calls from the car while he was driven to the office – many were the crackling gossips from the back seat, cut off at a tantalizing point as the car went under a bridge, to be resumed where they had broken off; on buying shirts en masse from Turnbull and Asser, any colour so long as it was white, and hand-made shoes. For longer journeys, flying, in England by helicopter, across the Atlantic by Concorde, was his preferred transport.

He liked spending "serious money" on modern art and from the mid-1980s he built up a collection of modern, mainly British, pictures impressive in its scope and quality. He set about collecting in his chosen area with characteristic thoroughness: he cultivated an "eye", he found out what he could about favourite artists such as Keith Vaughan, in particular, Prunella Clough, both then, as now, underrated; Kitaj, then, as now, over-rated, John Minton, Matthew Smith and Sickert.

Just as he had told his architects that he wanted "the best house in London", so now he set about filling it with the "best" collection of modern art; the pictures he bought suited the high, bare walls of the erstwhile studio, particularly those of the artist who formed the mainstay of his collection. Like Sebastian, Keith Vaughan, 1912-1977, a self-taught artist, had been a patient and friend of Patrick Woodcock, who introduced Sebastian to his work.

For Sebastian "there were shared and obvious sensibilities with Vaughan," as Grey Gowrie observed. Sebastian's Keith Vaughans, although predominantly homoerotic, were oddly unsensuous; often angular, black, tense, as compositions they were strong and well-defined. While Vaughan concerned himself with the male form he did not glorify it. His male nudes have a feeling of apartness, even of self-loathing. Sebastian responded also to their lack of elaboration, their paring away and their intensity.

Vaughan was undervalued and Sebastian made a donation towards the publication of his biography by Malcolm Yorke: "…behind Walker's munificence lay considerable shrewdness: if the book succeeded in boosting the reputation of Vaughan it would do no harm to the value of his collection," wrote Valerie Grove.

Sebastian's doctor and close friend, Patrick Woodcock, who introduced him to the paintings of Keith Vaughan. Right: Interior of Sebastian's house in Holland Park showing some of his collection, including (next to the window) "The Large Standing Figure", oil painting by Keith Vaughan, and (left) "Antigone" by Peter Lanyon, 1962

On Sebastian's balcony stood "Two Forms with White" (Greek) by Barbara Hepworth, cast in 1969

Sebastian's old friends Grey Gowrie, then the chairman of Sotheby's auction house, and his wife, Neite, lived opposite Sebastian in the mews. Lord Gowrie introduced him to the work of Vaughan's contemporary, Roger Hilton, several of whose paintings he bought. These artists' palettes were in the main subdued. Paradoxically, the most sensual picture in Sebastian's collection was a glorification of the female nude, a half-length figure by Matthew Smith. The artist Robert Medley, from whom he also bought a painting, drew his attention to this canvas. It was in the possession of Stephen Spender's family, who sold it to him. In 1982 Sebastian had asked Spender's son, Matthew, also an artist, for advice on investing in modern art. He gave him some good advice on: "How to Invest £100,000 a Year in Art Intelligently. Make friends with the artists. Get to know their colleagues. Listen to what they have to say about painting, for all reputations are based ultimately on the remarks painters make about each other. Allow them to choose their own works for you. When they are at the bottom, they will choose what they think is their best work. When they are at the top, the opposite is true."

As Grey Gowrie pointed out, Sebastian's pictures "are not decorative and they are not status symbols"; he bought lesser-known artists, such as Prunella Clough, as well as having "the means to buy artists with an international following, as the fine Kitaj and the Auerbachs and Kossoffs show. But he never bought for effect or fashion. If a work did not attract, in the way of a love affair almost, at an emotional level, it was sent back, however suitable it must have seemed in the context of the collection."

Luckily he had plenty of room on his walls for such canvasses as *Value, Price and Profit* by R.B. Kitaj which was five foot square; he bought this for £105,000 in 1985. (Incidentally it was sold from his collection at auction with exactly that estimate six years later.) In 1988 he acquired, for $165,217.39, another large canvas by R.B. Kitaj, entitled *The Londonist*. It showed a London cabbie reading a paperback of Henry James and the artist had this to say about it: "Life goes on beyond art but supposes a passage through art, across one's art… The man I call the Londonist is a taxi driver I only know slightly, by the name of Joey. He claims to be an American, born and

Tony Cragg's granite sculpture, "Yard", which visitors had to negotiate in order to climb upstairs in Sebastian's house in Holland Park

raised in Eastern Europe… I drew Joey as a Londonist, as an alien original thinker-cabbie, a big city Diasporist icon apotheosizing London's history as a refuge for oddballs." For a man who hated the pretentious as much as Sebastian did this choice of artist seemed strangely out of character.

As for sculpture, he bought a graceful William Turnbull abstract bronze, *Totem*, which now stands in the entrance hall of Walker Books; two bronze shapes by Barbara Hepworth, entitled *Two Forms with White* (Greek) were on the little balcony outside the studio window. He bought these for £144,000 in April 1990.

Sebastian was tolerant of visitors' comments along the lines of "I could have painted that!" or "What's that supposed to be?"; he enjoyed the discomfiture of those who found that the six foot square Roger Hilton canvas of a dripping phallic shape loomed rather uncomfortably over the dining table. He was amused to see people skirting the hefty granite sculpture by Tony Cragg in the hall in their efforts to get upstairs.

Entitled "Yard", this composition resembled a gun emplacement: its silent message was "Keep Out."

The Diagnosis

Sebastian was diagnosed HIV positive in the autumn of 1989. This faced him with many cruel decisions. Most immediately, should he keep his condition a secret? What would be the fate of Walker Books? It had always been very much his own creation – there was no board of directors, for example.

For some time Sebastian had feared he might be ill with this fatal disease which had begun to claim one or two of his contemporaries. He delayed taking the test as long as possible. Still the half-expected positive diagnosis came as a terrible blow. Sebastian was not used to being beaten. If something was amiss he strained every nerve to change it. But this illness was something over which he had no control. He put up a tremendous fight, mustering his prodigious willpower in his determination to prolong his life. Depression frequently overcame him as his strength steadily ebbed. One of the many cruel aspects of HIV and AIDS is the impossibility of predicting the pattern the illness will take, or the rate at which it will advance towards death.

Sebastian's doctor was Marisa Viegas, successor to Patrick Woodcock, who on retirement had gone to live for part of the year in France (much to Sebastian's fury). Dr Viegas was to attend Sebastian devotedly throughout the time left to him.

There is no medical treatment as such for AIDS. Each part of the body is treated as it becomes affected, the eyes, for instance, and the skin being commonly afflicted. The only remedy available was AZT (Azidothymidine) developed by Wellcome Pharmaceutical, which was meant to delay the progression of the disease.

"AZT spelled hope: psychologically it served to dispel despair. It was never claimed to be a cure but it bought extra time for people taking it before they became ill," wrote the journalist Simon Garfield in *The Independent on Sunday*, four years later.

AZT has since been shown to be ineffectual: "It made no difference either to mortality rates or to disease progression if one took AZT before the onset of AIDS." Even though its side effects were debilitating, predominant among them fatigue, nausea, depression, those who were HIV positive often preferred to take it. To take some medicine, rather than just live in fear of the onset of AIDS,[1] at least gave them a feeling of being to some extent in control of their own bodies, their own destiny. Sebastian was one of these. He went on to AZT, which is administered by the patients themselves, in his case through a tube in his chest. He immediately looked ghastly and felt worse, and eventually came off it, as it was not helping him.

The question of whether or not to let it be known that he was HIV positive was never satisfactorily resolved. Sebastian was the least discreet of people, but he was also a businessman, and for the bachelor founder of the most successful children's publishing house to be known to be dying of a sexually transmitted disease would not be good for business. There was still a long way that he wanted to take Walker Books in the time left to him – most importantly to secure its financial future – and he was

1 Background information from "The Rise and Fall of AZT" by Simon Garfield. *The Independent on Sunday* (May 2 1993) and *Retrovir* (market name for AZT) pamphlet produced by The Wellcome Foundation, 1988

determined that it should remain the buoyant company that it had always conspicuously been.

Maurice Sendak had called Sebastian "a kind of Prospero" but this illness and its inevitable outcome was not something he could magic away. Soon after the diagnosis Sendak stayed with Sebastian in London. He was someone from whom Sebastian had no secrets. This is his poignant account of what followed.

"He looked so sad. We had planned that he would come to Edinburgh with me. We were at his house and we were talking and there was something really wrong, and I remember I stood up and I said, 'Sebastian, you're very sick' and he burst into tears … and he was greatly relieved by crying and that I knew. I don't know how I knew; I didn't know that he was sick with that, I just knew that something was desperately wrong and I felt that it was a body ailment.

"There were no symptoms yet – he was just HIV at that point – it was just terror. He hadn't come to any philosophical attitudes about it yet, and he made a decision which I did not approve of at all: that it should be a secret – but the secret was to be so burdensome. We all kept the secret because he required it, but I didn't like it because he was so sick and this was a double burden, to be sick and to keep it a secret. It seemed to me he was putting a special problem on himself. I think he began to care less as he got sicker." This was to be the case; until then, Sebastian wanted to live as normal a life as possible, without people making concessions because he was ill. His innate fear of rejection made him afraid of being shunned by the largely heterosexual society in which he moved. In one way it was more complicated, in another way less, to keep his condition a secret. Most, but not all, of his intimate friends knew.

That autumn afternoon, in Edinburgh, Sebastian and Maurice walked to King Arthur's Seat. "He said something to the effect that how perverse it was of nature that I at my age should go on living and that he should die: it was not said with cruelty – under normal circumstances the older generation goes first.

"I said, 'You're being silly, because I've a heart condition, I can croak at any time, anything can happen to me,' and he said, I can hear his voice, 'Well, of course, it won't, will it, you will continue to live. Maurice, you can look over your shoulder and where you should have seen a whole bunch of people in back of you, pushing you off the mountain, you see no one because they're all dead.' And it's true, a whole generation has gone. That middle range is decimated, because of AIDS, that generation of thirty- and forty-year-olds. They were trapped in the early 1980s in their full sexual maturity, and he said, 'You've got the whole thing to yourself; I'm one of those too.'

"I said, 'Would you like me to run in front of a tram? Would that cheer you up if you went home all by yourself and said 'I'm still here; Maurice has gone'?

"But he was not going to have me make a joke of it. The message was that I had a special obligation, that I would have to continue the work that people like Sebastian and some few others had started. That I was spared and that as long as I lived I would have to think of him and of other people like him and do their work and it was a kind of plea because he felt terribly that he was superior and could do superior things and this had been taken away arbitrarily from him. So I had to do something for him. Sebastian could get away with that. Anyone else saying it would have been so painful, hurtful, but it wasn't.

"I thought afterwards that it was like two soldiers on the battlefield and one was mortally wounded and telling the other to continue, to make it to the end, except that I was the soldier who was going to make it, and the queer part of it was that I was the older of the two and he was the younger: it should have been the other way round, and did I realize the responsibility it put on me? That's what he was saying, and I did, I did. I'm continuing to the other side of the battlefield. I know it sounds very grandiose.

"One thing which it does which is most remarkable, it dissipates personal anxiety. I really feel it helped me psychologically. You like to pretend to yourself that you're carrying Sebastian on your back … there'll be many others, I'll be like a camel, but I'm willing to do it because I profit from it also. I've been working so hard and I've never been so happy in my life!"

This perversion of the natural order – the older generation of men remaining while he was to die – was to haunt Sebastian often during these last months of his life.

Meanwhile, at least Sendak was working on a long-cherished dream of Sebastian's, a book with Iona Opie for Walker Books. It was the first time for over twenty years that he had illustrated a text other than his own. *I Saw Esau* was a collection of over 170 rhymes, first published without illustrations by Iona and Peter Opie in 1947. In her introduction to this new edition, Iona Opie described how she gave Sebastian the one remaining copy which he put "in his pocket (it measures seven inches by five inches) and flew it across the Atlantic to show to Maurice Sendak. Maurice liked it; and there in the foyer of the Algonquin Hotel it was transferred to Maurice's pocket." After such a long interval since its first publication some rhymes had to be dropped, others inserted: "Amelia Edwards made a special copy of this new version for Maurice to carry around in his pocket wherever he went. He could scribble on the pages and fill in the spaces whenever he felt like it."

He enjoyed illustrating these rhymes which pinpoint children's anarchic sense of humour, and as he sent his pictures over from America, Amelia would show them to Sebastian. She made a point of going in to see him every day in his office, or taking pictures round to show him at home. Although he did not live to see the published result, he was delighted with the work in progress, and even contributed a rhyme to the book, one

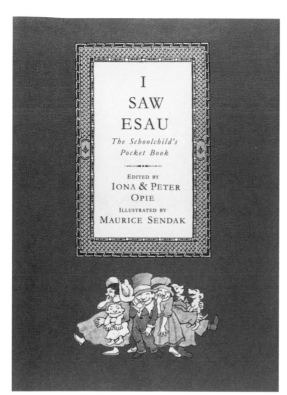

which had been thought endlessly funny when we were schoolchildren:

Je suis-
I am
A pot of jam.
Tu es —
Thou art
A juicy fart.

As Iona Opie wrote in her Introduction to the book, which was published in 1992, "The best antidote to the anxieties and disasters of life is laughter; and this children seem to understand almost as soon as they are born. If laughter is lacking, they create it; if it is offered to them, they relish it. Here in this book is a feast of laughter…

"It is a help, this book, in our universal predicament. We find we are born, so we might as well stay and do as well as we can; and while we are here we can at least enjoy the endearing absurdities of humankind."

Frontispiece (left) showing Sendak's drawing of himself (top right), Sebastian (top left), Iona Opie and her late husband, Peter, and (above) book cover

*Sebastian with
author and illustrator
Shirley Hughes
and his devoted
personal assistant,
Jenny Moores, at the
House of Commons,
1991*

The Last Summer, 1990

For a time Sebastian, pondering the future of Walker Books, contemplated selling it to become part of a larger organization. He could easily have done so since it was highly profitable. But he had never liked corporations, had always poured scorn on them: "I received a visit not long ago from a charming American, unknown to me, whom I understood wished to publish some of our books in the USA. It turned out he wanted to buy the company on behalf of a French group. I felt it uncivil, since he had come such a long way, to dismiss him summarily, so we talked for fifty minutes, me feeling bored and becoming rather depressed" – how well all who knew him remember that mood. "That afternoon Penny Dale brought in her illustrations for Martin Waddell's book *Rosie's Babies,* which were so utterly glorious that for three hours I was in an orbit of excitement.

"This incident taught me all I needed to know about my relationship with my authors and the capital value of Walker Books, which now has an annual turnover of £18 million," he wrote in an article in *The Sunday Telegraph* in May 1990. "A new book by Martin Handford, Helen Oxenbury, Shirley Hughes, Jill Murphy, Nicola Bayley or Barbara Firth, to name but a few of my authors and illustrators, is a million times more exciting than millions."

His objections to international publishing conglomerates were chiefly that they forgot the poor old authors: "They scythe off the author's rightful earnings like danegeld, they also present the author with a kind of antiseptic tank staffed by a corps de ballet of Managing Directors and people with other resonant Ruritanian titles."

Sebastian's solution to the future of Walker Books was much more visionary. In a move unique in the annals of publishing he

created a discretionary Trust, to which he gave away 51% of the company, the beneficiaries of which are Walker Books employees, authors and illustrators. In this way he prevented all that he had worked to create over the last decade being eaten up by tax after his imminent death. Sebastian retained 49% of the shares and remained Chairman.

Martin Waddell, Sebastian and Penny Dale at the Parents Magazine Best Books for Babies Award, 1990

Naturally this caused a stir in publishing circles. He "has created a fairy tale for his staff, authors and illustrators," commented *The Financial Times*. There was sniping, too, as *The Sunday Times* reported: "'I haven't worked out what the catch is,' says Tom Maschler, his former boss at Cape, sourly, 'but I'm sure there is a catch somewhere.'" This was a characteristic dig from a jealous rival who had been grinding his teeth impotently throughout Sebastian's successful career.

In *The Sunday Telegraph* Sebastian explained that book publishing "has all but forgotten its most crucial element: the authors themselves.

"A publishing house does nothing else but publish authors' work. It can therefore have no other source of income. By owning 51% of the company one guarantees that decisions affecting the ownership of the company can only be in the best interest of the authors and employees – and therefore their work.

"If a publishing house is sold or goes public, or pays dividends, surely 51% at least of these should go to the authors, illustrators and key employees whose work earned the money in the first place.

Harry Gould,
Sebastian's long-
established financial
advisor, who was
instrumental in
setting up The
Walker Books
Employee Trust
in 1990

"Obviously no company or publishing house can function without an operating profit with which to innovate, take risks, and pay for the misses, all of it earned from the hits. But as the years go by all this profit and endeavour contribute to the capital value of a publishing house. And, as I said, what does a publishing house do but publish authors' work?"

Brave words, which it must have been difficult for Sebastian to write, knowing why he had to secure the future of his cherished company. A week before, to his old friend Valerie Grove in *The Sunday Times*, he had put up a brilliantly insouciant performance: under the headline "Publishing Wizard Casts a Sweet Spell of Success" alongside a picture of Sebastian with an enchanting baby girl belonging to one of his employees and a Wally book in the background, with the caption "Writers' friend: 'Authors aren't stupid. They go to the publisher who designs their books best and sells the most,' says Walker."

As a piece of public relations for Walker Books at this critical juncture it was faultless: "He is a charming companion, ordering the best champagne in immaculate French and then seizing the bill ('I'm so rich, and poor Mr Murdoch has all those debts.')."

The Bookseller (April 27, 1990) hinted at the pressing reason for setting up the Trust but did not develop it: "The Trust secures the independence of the company should Mr Walker die. If that had happened under the previous arrangement the company would have had to be sold to pay death duties. The transfer, because it benefits employees, doesn't attract any capital gains tax."

The impression given was of a man whose success and longevity were assured. Walker Books had never been more successful: turnover was over £17 million for the previous year, with profits topping £1 million. The first payment to the beneficiaries of the Trust, on March 1, 1991, was £1,000 to each of 104 authors, illustrators and key employees. The Trust was discretionary, with two trustees, appointed by Sebastian – his accountant and long-time friend, Harry Gould, and his lawyer, Andrew Stone, both of whom had helped him to set it up and to make his financial affairs watertight.

In addition, Sebastian created a board of directors to ensure the stable management of Walker Books after his death: of the six directors, five had been part of his original team, and the sixth, David Heatherwick, Financial Director, had joined Walker Books just over a year previously. All of them, of course, knew that he was mortally ill.

In another show of solidarity, Walker Books threw a tenth anniversary party in June 1990. The mattress factory was transformed with candles and flowers. Sebastian stood at the door to greet his guests, a slightly forlorn figure, in his immaculate white dinner jacket, flanked by an equally immaculate David Ford, who did the smiling and nodding for him. Guests sat down to dinner at little round tables: here was the cream of the children's book world. There were speeches, there was dancing, congratulations for Sebastian on his decade of success and good wishes for many more years to come. How few of his guests that evening knew that he had only a year more to live!

The following month, Sebastian travelled to Annecy to say farewell to the Davignon family, who had first introduced him to France as a schoolboy of fifteen. They did not know that he was ill, neither did his travelling companion, Simone Warner; he was healthy-looking but subdued. "I really respected Sebastian. Although he was depressed a lot of the

David Heatherwick, the financial director of Walker Books, who gave Sebastian sound advice during the difficult last months and (below) Quentin Blake's birthday card, 1990

time he didn't put that depression on to me," says Simone. They drove together southwards from Normandy over several days.

Sebastian had always kept up with the Davignon family; Madame wrote him regular letters assuring him of *"notre fidèle*

amitié". Now he had arranged to take Monsieur and Madame with Jean-François, his original exchange, now a lawyer in his mid-forties, and his wife, out to lunch at the celebrated Auberge au Père Bise, at Talloires, a few kilometres from Annecy. Belonging to Paul Bocuse, it has two rosettes in the Michelin guide, and one can eat outside on a shady terrace overlooking the lake.

Sebastian reunited with the Davignon family in Annecy hotê-Savoire. From left, Jean-François, his French exchange as a schoolboy; Sebastian; Simone Warner; and Madame Davignon

"It was clearly a very big thing for him," says Simone Warner. "We got to Annecy the night before and we went and looked at the restaurant and the menu, not to order anything, just to see what there was.

"Next day we sat outside on the terrace waiting

for them; Sebastian had asked them for twelve and they were a little late, and he began to get a bit worried in case something had gone wrong.

"Anyway they duly arrived, and Sebastian had ordered a very special champagne for them. Madame was now eighty and you could see what a fine-looking woman she had been. She had a strong face and a good skin, she was *bien coiffée* and she wore a silk dress. There was an almost tangible affection between her and Sebastian.

"There was a certain formality between them as well, a great respect from Sebastian towards her. They had a running joke that she was still allowed to correct his French as she had done all those years ago."

It was a splendid farewell to the person who had introduced him to the country where he felt most at home, whose language he was fluent in and whose food he adored. The schoolboy Madame Davignon had first met, curly-haired and wide-eyed, was now prodigiously successful, and generous enough to give her a sumptuous treat. There was no trace of sadness in that meeting. "Sebastian completely forgot himself," continued Simone. "There was terrific chatter about times past. They were all tremendously greedy, we had a wonderful meal of five courses, including individual lobster soufflés and a champagne sorbet in the middle.

"No one ever drew breath: at five o'clock there was a sudden extraordinary thunderstorm. We didn't move but went on sitting under the plane trees until the water started dripping through the leaves. Then we went inside and Sebastian suggested we had tea.

"They left about half past five, and after we had waved them off in their car Sebastian turned to me and said, 'Do you think they enjoyed themselves?'"

Madame Davignon died that November, Sebastian the following year.

The End

For a brief while a nursery was set up on the ground floor of Walker Books. "We do not say 'crèche' here, there is a perfectly good English word," pronounced Sebastian.

"If you are going to take women staff seriously you must accept that they have babies." The trouble was that they began breeding at such a rate that many of them were constantly off on maternity leave. So that experiment had to come to an end; instead, mothers received an allowance towards their choice of childcare.

There were other, more crucial, company decisions to be made by Sebastian while he still had time to make them. He had to streamline Walker Books, which meant shedding the loss-making affiliated imprints, Nick Hern and Julia MacRae. All too swiftly these turned into prima donna sackings with tears and rows and recriminations. Sebastian was in too much haste to be tactful and feeling too emotionally raw himself to take others' emotions into account.

Immediately after that, in August, he went to stay with his family in Norfolk. For him it was not a happy visit. He was emotionally drained, his nerves on edge, withdrawn and unhappy. Still he enjoyed an expedition to lunch at The Moorings restaurant with his nephews and nieces, punctuated as usual by a visit to the rock shop across the road. In many ways their ignorance of his illness was a help, because they continued to treat him just as their delightful, eccentric Uncle Sebby, not as a dying man. Besides, he still looked healthy, plump and pink. Only those who knew him really detected the sadness and ill health. He had put on weight, saying that as long as he was plump he could not have AIDS.

Within a short while of Sebastian's return to London, Dr Viegas had installed him in hospital for a complete rest. Staring out of the window at a helicopter skimming across Chelsea Bridge, "Look!" he said, "that's what I want to get next! And have WALKER BOOKS on the side!"

As a recuperative holiday he went to Munich afterwards with Freda Berkeley, to whom he had remained a close friend for over twenty years, to stay with equally long-standing friends, the illustrator Binette Schroeder and her husband Peter Nickl.

There were two exciting projects at Walker Books which he had put in hand although he did not expect to see them come to fulfilment: both were dear to his heart. For years he had wanted to publish a children's magazine: SNAP! was aimed at five- to eight-year-olds. An editorial team was formed, under the guidance of David Lloyd; the editor was Lucy Ingrams.

The other idea was to start an American imprint of Walker Books. This would be called Candlewick Press (not after the curious ridged material beloved of landladies in the 1950s but after the candle the Walker bear carries). David Ford found premises near Boston, in Cambridge, Massachusetts. Sadly, Sebastian never saw the finished results of either of these two pioneering ventures, nor did he visit David Ford while he was setting up in America, but he was pleased that Walker Books was going to build up a presence there, even in a recession.

He had now done everything he could to secure the company's future by creating a board of directors and the artists' and authors' Trust; by paring down Walker Books to owning just its own imprint; by putting SNAP! and Candlewick Press in train. Although his strength was ebbing, he was determined to keep coming into the office as long as he could, for when he gave that up, he gave up everything. Still, his illness was kept from all but a handful of people at Walker Books.

In the spring of 1991 he and his directors went for a final weekend together to the Isles of Scilly. Here on the green island of Tresco, surrounded by their faces familiar for the eleven years since he founded Walker Books on their shared energy, determination and talent, he was, briefly, happy, tranquil, even. Yet he was far from being reconciled to death, to

Freda Berkeley,
Binette Schroeder
and Sebastian,
Munich, 1990

183

abandoning his enterprise to its own fate. "You can't imagine what it means to leave all this," he said to me in a rare moment of intimacy, waving his arm round his office.

Sebastian and his directors on their way to Tresco for a final weekend together

Now his capacity to imagine, to fantasize, which had stood him in good stead as a far-sighted publisher, got the better of him. He imagined himself dying alone, rejected, abandoned by his family and friends, incontinent, or blind, or mad, or all of these. The horror of AIDS is that, apart from the inevitability of death, none of its symptoms are inevitable, or predictable. Still, the weaker Sebastian felt himself becoming, the more he fought. His doctor, his personal assistant, Jenny Moores, his driver, Noel, and his friends, all organized his life to make it as easy as possible for him; a Chinese housekeeper, Ping, came to look after him, softly shuffling about the studio in her slippers. She cooked wonderful Chinese meals which nourished him – he had not, at least, lost his relish for food. His nephews and nieces, who had by now been told how ill he was, wrote to him and came to see him. For the last time he went abroad with his dear friend Patrick Woodcock; they went to Spain, and Patrick's company was as always soothing and solicitous. Sebastian felt secure with him. Across the mews Grey and Neite Gowrie were welcoming and watchful … countless friends rang and visited … and yet … and yet … to be thus dependent on their coming to him did not suit him. As always he "put the shutters up" at a certain stage, wanting to let people only so far into his life. The loneliness people detected about him was ambiguous: a lot of it was a genuine liking for his own company and an impatience with too much of other people's.

In the grip of this deadly illness, his hold on life was incredible: almost defiantly, as if to spite death, he made plans to rent a house on Jura, in the Scottish islands. In June he was invited for the weekend to Badminton, by the Duchess of Beaufort. Somehow he managed to go for the last time to a house he loved and where he had spent many happy Christmases. Now the roses were in bloom and he could admire them through the window without being able to walk much in the garden.

Some days later, on Wednesday, June 12, he was examined by the brain specialist who had been seeing him regularly, and who pronounced that the lesions on his brain were going to increase. Knowing that this meant eventual deterioration of his brain, Sebastian finally admitted defeat. He refused all further medication.

He invited us to visit him two days later, on Friday, June 14, at 6.00 p.m. We brought some roses from the garden. He was lying peacefully in bed, gentler and more at ease with himself than he had been for many months. Ping glided in and arranged the roses on the bedside table. We knew we were unlikely to see one another again, and yet nothing disturbed his composure. We chatted about our plans: I told him we were going to Rome the following week, "in theory at least". "What do you mean, in theory?" he demanded. Ashamed to admit that all plans were tentative given his illness, I said that of course we were going; but I didn't venture on the artificial hope that he might come too…

Suddenly after painful months of strain and misunderstanding we had everything to talk about: Hans Christian Andersen, whose *Snow Queen* I was reading to my youngest daughter, and why his stories, which were often archaically written, nevertheless are more successful than, say, *Thomas the Tank Engine*: "That's because they touch a child's imagination," said Sebastian.

"And now, I think…" turning his head away on the pillow.

"Yes, we must leave you to sleep…" we said, getting up.

"My trouble is not *getting* to sleep…"

"…but waking up!" we said, simultaneously.

"We'll talk on Monday," we said, all of us knowing that we wouldn't; we smiled and I waved at him from the bedroom door uplifted against all expectation by this last meeting with my brother. From then on he would not see anybody except Dr Viegas and Ping.

He slept, but would not eat, Ping told us, alarmed that for the first time her delicious food was going untouched. On Sunday afternoon, just after five o'clock we called round to Holland Park Road. The doctor met us; Sebastian had died fifteen minutes previously.

We went up to see him. He lay as if asleep, his head fallen, childlike, against the pillow. I held his hand; it was still warm, and soft. I kissed his cheek. He seemed a young man again, his face untroubled. In his white bedroom, hung with the pictures he loved, he died as he had wanted to, since die he must, alone, and at peace.

This book is dedicated

to those of my brother's generation,

the first to be ravaged by AIDS,

who have borne their

illness with an inspiring bravery.

M.C.

Picture Credits

*I would like to thank everyone
who granted me permission to use
photographs, and gratefully
acknowledge the following. I apologize
if any photographers have been
inadvertently omitted.*

pp 10, 13, 14: Sebastian and Mirabel
as children by their father   p. 28:
Selina Hastings by Frances Charteris
p. 30: Iris Murdoch by Frances
Charteris   p. 35: Jude and Alex de
Jonge by Patrick Lichfield for *Vogue*
p. 37: Sebastian by Robert Penn   p.
44: Virginia Ironside by Carole
Latimer   p. 45: Virginia and
Sebastian by West End Photo Service
p. 47: Sebastian and his father by
Frances Charteris
p. 50: Clare Toynbee by Patrick
Lichfield for *Vogue*   p. 55: Wedding
photographs by Frances Charteris
p. 56: Sidney Walker by Frances
Charteris   p. 57: Sir Lennox and
Lady Berkeley by Frank Herrmann
for *The Sunday Times*   p. 58:
Sebastian by Christina Gascoigne
p. 60: Watercolour of Chatto &
Windus by John Ward RA,
photographed by Richard Holt, with
thanks to Hugo Brunner   p. 72:
Amelia Edwards by John Vigurs
p. 75: Wendy Boase by John Vigurs
p. 77: Helen Oxenbury by Carole
Cutner   p. 79: Helen Oxenbury and
daughter Emily by Gary Weaser for

The Guardian   p. 94: Sebastian by
Carole Cutner   p. 100: Hugh Cecil
by Richard Holt   p. 102: Sebastian
at his piano for *Harpers & Queen*
p. 104: Sebastian's "bed-sitting-
room" for Sotheby's   p. 107: Joanna
Steichen by Thomas Victor
p. 117: Amy Ehrlich by Tom Gilson
p. 122: "The Moorings" by
Brian Lewis, reproduced courtesy of
the artist   p. 124: Photographs by
Richard Holt; old photograph kindly
supplied by Harry Gould   p. 131:
Iona Opie by Jeremy Young   p. 140:
William Mayne by Carole Cutner;
Patrick Benson by Perry Ogden
p. 141: Selina Hastings by John
Vigurs; Juan Wijngaard by Carole
Cutner   p. 142: Martin Waddell by
Terry Bowman   p. 146: Colin
McNaughton by Michael Ann
Mullen   p. 147: Angela Barrett by
Michael Owen   p. 148: Sebastian
by David Gamble for *The Observer*
p. 151: Vivien Banfield by Richard
Holt   p. 153: Tatayana Nikolaieva
by Alex von Koettlitz/P.A.L   p. 156:
Julia Hodgkin by Richard Holt
p. 159: Holland Park Road for
Sotheby's   p. 160: "Two Forms
with White" by Barbara Hepworth
for Sotheby's   p. 162: Tony Cragg
"Yard" for the Lissom Gallery
by Sue Ormorod   p. 164: Sebastian
by John Hilton   p. 172: Sebastian,
Shirley Hughes and Jenny Moores
by Jean Fraser   p. 174: Martin
Waddell, Sebastian and Penny Dale
by Martin Cole

The text of this book was
typeset by the publishers in
11/13 Monotype Bembo.

The cover design and
lettering are by Ken Wilson.

The front and back jacket
photographs are taken from
the author's personal album.

The author's photograph on
the back flap was taken by
Richard Holt.

Computer reprographic
services by The London
Black & White Company.

Printed in Great Britain
by Clays Ltd, St Ives plc

Published 1995 by
Walker Books Ltd
87 Vauxhall Walk,
London SE11 5HJ

British Library Cataloguing
in Publication Data
A catalogue record for this
book is available from the
British Library.

ISBN 0-7445-4423-8